Navigating the Newborn Months and Beyond:
A Mother's Guide to Routine, Sleep, Fussiness, and Self-Care
Copyright © 2021 by Erin Eileen Leigh
All rights reserved.

Published in the United States by Erin Eileen Leigh

Library of Congress number: TXu 2-292-603

Cover design by Fiona Jayda Media https://fionajaydemedia.com/

Edited by Jessica L. Andersen https://jessicalandersen.com/

Formatted by Kate Burnett https://wordartistry.com.au/

ISBN: 978-0-578-36186-4

For my loves, Greysen McCauley, Asher Morgan, Savannah Eileen, and Beckett Brooks. You gave me ten years of ideas and inspiration for this book.

INTRODUCTION

"Being a mother is rewarding to one's female instincts, trying to one's nerves, physically exhausting, emotionally both frustrating and satisfying and above all, not to be undertaken lightly."

— DR. MARGARET RAPHAEL

Motherhood has been the most rewarding and amazing experience of my life. It has also been the most challenging experience of my life. As a mother of a newborn, you may harbor self-doubt about caring for and raising a child. I know I did. I still remember the drive home from the hospital with our first child. We walked into our home and set down the infant car seat, with the baby sleeping soundly, in the middle of the family room and looked at each other. I remember my husband saying to me, "So, what do we do now?" Despite all the parenting books I read, I felt self-doubt approaching like a steamroller on that first evening home. You may experience similar feelings of self-doubt, but you will find that you are more than capable of caring for your baby. Like every other parent, you will learn by trial and error each day. You may, as I did, discover ways to make some of the challenges of motherhood less overwhelming to you.

I waited ten years after getting married to start a family. Frankly, most of our family members had given up on the possibility of any babies from us and assumed we would not have children. I knew I wanted to have children, but I was nervous and uncertain about how it would change my life. Once I was ready to embark on the journey of parenting, there were several topics that I wanted to explore and understand. The first was how motherhood would affect my daily schedule and routine. When I was pregnant, I knew there would be significant changes to my current routine and schedule. However, I was unsure how much my routine would change and precisely *what* things would change. I wanted to keep some things that were important to me in my day-to-day schedule. Would I still be able to do the activities that I enjoyed doing? If so, how often and when? How could I plan anything when I had a newborn who would be unpredictable and need my constant attention? As someone who likes to plan ahead and have regularity, I wanted answers to these questions and was determined to create a routine that supported my needs and those of my baby.

The second topic on my mind when I was pregnant was sleep. I was nervous about how the lack of sleep during the newborn phase would affect me. I witnessed friends and family appear exhausted when their children were babies. I wondered about how much sleep I would actually get when I had a newborn. Would it be a *little* less than normal or a lot less than normal? I behave like a better human being when I have more than a few hours of sleep. A couple nights of lost sleep periodically are one thing, but the idea of having weeks (or months!) of minimal sleep terrified me.

Once I had my first baby, sleep was still a constant thought on my mind (and it may be for you too). *When will I sleep next? How many hours of sleep will I get? Will the baby sleep and when? Will I able to sleep when the baby sleeps? How does a new mother function properly with only two or three hours of sleep for five or six (or more) consecutive weeks?* I did not want to give up most of my sleep for the next ten years if I could avoid it. I knew I needed to find solutions to these concerns.

The third subject that occupied my mind when I was pregnant, and in the first few weeks after I had my first baby, was how motherhood would affect my mental and physical health. Self-care is important to me, and I wanted to make sure I found ways to maintain my physical and mental health. Would I have any time for myself? How could I maintain my sense of self while also learning to develop my new role as a mother? Before becoming a mom, I was an attorney. Although I was comfortable switching to a limited part-time position, I was uncertain how I would feel about this change long-term and whether it would be fulfilling for me. I enjoy hiking, running, swimming, traveling, playing the piano, and reading, and I wondered whether I would be able to continue some or all of these activities. Would I have personal time for myself to socialize with friends or have a date night with my husband? I knew many things would change when I became a mother, but I was committed to taking care of myself and keeping my health a priority.

I am a mother of four children, three sons and one daughter, all spaced about two years apart. For a period of eight years, I was either pregnant or nursing. As a result, when my children were babies, I was always searching for ways to make my life easier and improve everyone's sleep. I am an avid reader and discovered there are countless books on babies, parenting, and sleep, and I read many of these books during pregnancy and in the first few months of motherhood. I found helpful suggestions in every book, but I always found myself with more questions than answers after finishing each book. I realized that I needed to create a guide based on my own research and experiences. After I had my first baby, I began journaling every day. I wrote down the ideas that worked for me and those that did not work well. I kept track of my son's nap times and feeding times and documented his transition stages. I think of transition stages as pivotal times when your baby is moving from one developmental phase to another, such as dropping a nap, weaning off the pacifier, rolling over during sleep, breaking out of a swaddle, and many more. I wrote about every transition phase and each milestone my babies achieved. I wrote about the challenges, victories, and frustrations of motherhood. I kept an ongoing list of my successful ideas. When I finally decided to write this book, I had four years of my own field research on babies documented in my journals.

I listened to many moms talk about their struggle with creating a routine, lack of sleep, frustration with their baby's fussiness, and carving out personal time for themselves. Other moms often asked me how I was able to find any time for myself. How was I able to create such a strong and consistent nap schedule? How did I have so much energy even when my children were babies, and I was not sleeping as much? As more moms asked me for advice, I felt compelled to share my experiences and ideas with other mothers.

My goal is to help you create a daily routine, maximize your baby's sleep, reduce your baby's fussiness, and prioritize self-care. Without a solid routine and self-care, you will find it difficult to achieve quality sleep, and your baby's sleep patterns will likely be unpredictable. The guidelines I share in this book helped me survive those first few months of infancy and truly cherish my time with my babies. Yes, there were stressful situations, difficult times, and sleepless nights. However, routine and organization helped me be a happier, less sleep-deprived mom and gave me more control over my life. I was able to accomplish so much more than I thought was possible once I took care of myself and followed the routine I created. I discovered that if I took care of myself, I was a better mom.

PART 1: CREATING YOUR DAILY ROUTINE

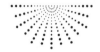

"Motherhood is wonderful, but it's also hard work. It's the logistics more than anything. You discover you have reserves of energy you didn't know you had."

— DEBORAH MAILMAN

It is never too soon to establish a routine when you have a baby. Having a routine helps you reduce stress and gain control over your life. In addition, routine enables you to develop a sense of confidence as a new mother. After your baby is two weeks old, it is time for you to take charge of your life and schedule. Otherwise, this new little person in your life will dictate everything you do. Everything. A baby requires almost constant attention and commands control over many aspects of your day. However, you can still have time for yourself to accomplish what you want to do. If you want to carve out personal time, it is important that you create a routine that supports your needs as well as those of your baby. As a mother, you will often face unexpected situations. You will discover that motherhood is a lifelong test of patience, adaptability, and flexibility. Having a routine will help you function more effectively each day and handle the ups and downs of motherhood.

1

THE TO-DO LIST

As a new mother, it may feel daunting to find a routine for you and your new baby. After all, you have just gone through a major life transition. Your newly defined role as a parent is to provide constant care and support for this tiny human being *and* take care of yourself and your household. With a newborn, you are responsible for your baby's basic needs for survival. That is a massive undertaking! Since your newborn baby is entirely dependent on you, your waking hours become a continuous cycle of your baby's feedings, diaper changes, and naps. In addition to your baby's needs, you must meet your own basic needs. You also have the daily responsibilities of your family and your household. You may have other children, a spouse, parents, or pets to support also.

When you enter the world of motherhood, your personal freedom becomes drastically minimized. Clinical psychologist Claire Nicogossian describes personal freedom as "your ability as a mom of finding ways of doing things that used to come with ease, such as taking a shower, using the bathroom, eating a meal, and getting out of the house in order to go to the supermarket, work, exercise, or spend time with your friends or partner."[1] At first, it may be challenging to find new ways to accomplish simple daily tasks and achieve some personal freedom, but you will learn how to adjust to your new role and life with each week that passes.

Creating a routine helps you cultivate more balance in your life and enables you to prioritize what tasks need to be done and when. Each day, there are tasks, appointments, meetings, and personal needs but not everything needs to be a priority. To begin creating a routine, think about the things you absolutely need and want to do and write down what you want to accomplish today. This is your to-do list.

I love to-do lists because they are easy and quick to make, and they keep us in check. According to psychologist and author Dr. David Cohen, creating to-do lists on paper is helpful for three reasons. First, it reduces anxiety about the chaos of life. Second, writing to-do lists gives us a structure and a plan that we can stick to. Third, paper to-do lists are proof of our achievements that day, week, or month.[2]

The science behind creating to-do lists is fascinating. There is a concept called the Zeigarnik effect, named after psychologist Bluma Zeigarnik, which you may have encountered if you have taken psychology courses. The Zeigarnik effect proposes that people remember unfinished tasks better than tasks that have been completed. Based on this theory, when you intend to complete a task by first putting it on a to-do list, you are more likely to remember that unfinished task. Every time you see your list, your brain has a quick reminder of what needs to be accomplished and focuses on what is unfinished.

My memory always served me well until I had children, and I was surviving on minimal sleep. Lack of sleep makes it difficult to remember all the tasks you need to accomplish and contributes to your frustration and stress. It can be challenging to focus when you are tired and caring for an infant. Creating a to-do list and using your list in order of priorities makes it easier for you to accomplish what you want to do each day.

A research study conducted by Dr. Gail Matthews at Dominican University of California considered different strategies for achieving goals.[3] One of the main conclusions from her work was that people who wrote down their goals were significantly more likely to achieve those goals. Whether it is a short-term or long-term goal, the process of making a list to achieve those goals is an effective tool. Writing something down makes it real and creates an extra reminder in your brain of what you need to do. It also makes it stand out as an incomplete task or unfinished work.

You may find that the act of writing down your tasks will make it easier for you to remember them. You can choose how you want to make your list. You can write it on a notepad, in a journal or notebook, in your phone or tablet, or on a whiteboard or bulletin board. Regardless of where you write your to-do list, it is important to keep your list in the same place every day. Put your list in a place where you will see it often throughout the day. I prefer to use whiteboards and notepads to keep track of my daily tasks and goals, but I also have an app on my phone for my various other ongoing lists (i.e., grocery, Target, Costco, house projects, etc.). In addition, I have a small whiteboard in my bathroom so I can jot things down first thing in the morning or before I go to bed. I also have a whiteboard and notepad in our kitchen, since I spend most of my time there, and I will see my list multiple times throughout the day. Some people prefer to use their phones or tablets to type or record a to-do list. This can work also if you include reminders for yourself and are able to cross off or otherwise clearly mark what you have completed. As I cross things off my list, I see the completed tasks and I am motivated to do even more.

Your to-do list does not need to be lengthy. In fact, when you begin making to-do lists, having three to four items on your list may be enough to get you started. Be realistic about what is manageable for you in this stage of your life. Making a to-do list helps you determine and focus on the things that are a priority to you. Instead of having a million thoughts jumbled and disorganized in your brain, a list helps you concentrate only on what you need to do that day.

As you make your to-do list, consider what you really *need* to accomplish each day. Then think about what you really *want* to accomplish

5

each day. Occasionally, these may be the same, but most likely, the things you want to do may differ from what you need to do. I encourage you to include tasks on your list that you need to do for your family and activities you want to do for your own well-being. Yes, it is acceptable (and encouraged) to do something for yourself! You will be amazed at how you are able to find time for what you want to do when you make it a priority by writing it down. Psychologist Barbara Fredrickson explains that people who prioritize positivity, such as by including things on their to-do lists that boost their positive emotions and mood, tend to be mentally healthier.[4] Whether it is taking time to have a nap, read a book, get your hair cut, call a friend, get coffee with a friend, or just go for a walk alone, it is essential to make time for yourself. Even a small window of time can do wonders for your emotional well-being. When you make an appointment, such as for a haircut or a doctor visit, find a way to keep your commitment. Sometimes, it may seem like a hassle to have to find a babysitter or another caregiver to help with your baby, but your self-care is worth the effort. By following through on your tasks and goals, you will feel accomplished.

It is helpful to rank things on your to-do list in order of importance *to you*. When you think about what you want to accomplish each day as a mom, these goals may be quite simple human needs, such as taking a nap, eating dinner with your spouse, or taking a shower. Some items on my list remained the same every day. Others changed daily. However, the goals I wanted to accomplish always included things for myself, not just tasks related to my baby. It is easy to make excuses and avoid what you want to accomplish. It is just as easy to make certain items a priority and create a realistic schedule for yourself so you can accomplish these tasks. It is up to you to decide what tasks and goals will enable you and your household to function most efficiently and effectively.

Below is an example of one of my to-do lists when my first baby was a few weeks old. If I was able to accomplish all (or even most) of the items on my list, I felt successful and better equipped to tackle the challenges of the next day. As I slept more and grew accustomed to my new schedule with my newborn son, I added more tasks to my to-do list.

1. Pump breast milk and wash all the baby bottles and pumping equipment (I wrote this first on the list because it was my *least* favorite task. I wanted to be finished with it as soon as possible.)
2. Exercise/go for a walk
3. Shower
4. Schedule appointments
5. Journal
6. Return phone calls and emails

Some of these items may seem like basic tasks that do not need to be written on a to-do list. However, think of these as steps or small goals in your daily plan. Before having children, it was not a problem for me to find time to shower every day, but with a baby, I had to make it a priority, or it might not happen. Would I remember these seemingly simple tasks if I did not write them down? Possibly. Would I be as likely to do them if I did not have a list that I saw throughout the day? Definitely not. Did I feel better about myself seeing what I had accomplished? Absolutely.

Use the format that works best for you, but whatever medium you choose, keep the list in a place where you will see it often. Seeing it will be a reminder of what you want to accomplish that day. Set yourself up for success.

There may be frustrating days when you do not accomplish all the tasks on your list or when everything you set out to do becomes reprioritized. That is fine. Give yourself a break. You have a baby, and you are doing the best you can. Remember that it is one day, and tomorrow is a new day. For example, you may, as I did, want to have a shower every day. Even when you make showering a priority, sometimes the baby is fussy or crying while you take a short shower either because her nap ended sooner than you anticipated, or she is unhappy sitting in the bouncer chair. However, a three-minute shower is better than no shower at all, and you will feel recharged and better because of it! In their book, Parenting is Wonder-full, Sue Miller and Holly Delich summarize motherhood with a newborn perfectly: "Today's actual accomplishments – kept one tiny human alive, clothed, fed, changed, rested and entertained."[5] Parenting a newborn is a full-time job, and every day that you care for your baby is an accomplishment. The goal of creating a to-do list and a routine is to help you feel balanced and organized. The intent is not to make yourself feel bad about what you did not accomplish, so be kind to yourself.

You may find that you need to give up certain activities or tasks that you did before having a child, maybe temporarily and maybe permanently. Some things you will miss, and some you may not. Having a child will challenge you to simplify certain areas of your life and determine what is truly important to you and your family. You may not have a quiet breakfast and coffee by yourself or with your significant other for many, many years. However, when you do have that coveted personal time, you will deeply appreciate that time for yourself. I discovered that sitting down for a meal is not overrated!

Create a to-do list that is realistic and achievable as a parent of a newborn. Making lists of tasks, even simple ones, also allows you to feel a sense of accomplishment when you cross each task off your to-do list. You will feel more productive and positive about yourself when you make a list of your tasks and goals each day.

2

YOUR DAILY SCHEDULE

CREATING A SCHEDULE THAT FITS YOUR NEEDS

When you have a newborn, you are tired. In fact, you may feel utterly and completely drained of energy. You are tired in the morning, and you only become more tired as the day goes on. You look at your to-do list and feel overwhelmed. How will you manage to complete the items on your list when you are so exhausted?

The answer is to create a schedule that fits your needs. You can start by focusing on how and when you will accomplish the tasks on your to-do list each day. This seems simple, but it is easy to get distracted and take a phone call, check emails, or clean up a mess somewhere in the house. If doing laundry is a priority on your to-do list, do that first. If there is still time, then make your phone calls or check emails. If your priority is taking a shower or making a certain phone call, do those things before sitting down in front of the computer. If you want to take a walk with your baby, plan out the best time to do that based on your baby's feeding and sleep schedule, and make that a priority.

According to behavioral scientist Dan Ariely, the first two hours of our day are likely to be our most productive if we use them to accomplish what we need to do.[1] Generally, I would not describe myself as a morning person. However, once I had my first baby, I realized I was much more productive if I completed tasks earlier in the day. Once it was late afternoon and early evening, I was drained and unmotivated to do much of anything. Whenever possible, do as much as you can in the morning before your energy level decreases.

Psychology writer Eric Barker recommends doing your most-dreaded tasks first, since your willpower becomes depleted as the day wears on.[2] Doing the tasks you dislike the most may not be how you envision starting your day. However, if there is a task you dread, consider doing it first so it is not hanging over your head for the remainder of the day. For example, I wanted to have plenty of extra milk stored in the freezer and a fresh bottle for a nighttime feeding, so pumping, storing, and freezing milk were priorities for me. However, pumping and washing pump parts were also my least-favorite tasks, and I wanted to complete them as soon as possible so I did not have to think about them the rest of the day. After my baby's first morning feeding, usually between 6:00 and 7:00 a.m., I would pump because this was when my milk supply was the highest. My least favorite task was completed before 8:00 a.m., and I could move forward with other things I wanted to accomplish that day.

Creating a schedule that works for you also involves finding the best windows of time to complete your tasks. For me, first thing in the morning and early afternoon were my most productive times. My baby usually had a long nap in the morning, so I knew this was my optimal window of time to get anything done. On a good day, I took a shower, put in a load of laundry, or did a few administrative tasks during this time. Other days, if my baby woke early from his nap and was fussy, spit up, or had a diaper explosion, my shower was short or had to wait until the baby's next nap. The laundry might become two loads due to the baby's spit-up. Having a backup plan and being flexible are the keys to accomplishing your goals. Instead of just giving up on your tasks, adjust your schedule and move a few things around. Some days, one or two things on your list will need to be reprioritized or postponed.

Being flexible means coming up with multiple solutions to accomplish your tasks. For example, I knew that if I wanted to take a shower every day, I had three options. I could shower when my baby was asleep in his crib. This was the ideal option, since it allowed me to have a peaceful shower uninterrupted. If my baby was awake, I could put him in the bouncer chair or on the play mat on the floor in the bathroom while I showered. The other option would be waiting until my husband returned at the end of the day, which was not appealing to me. As a result, nine times out of ten, I showered while my baby napped or sat in the bouncer chair next to the shower. I could still see and hear my baby and talk to him to soothe him when he was in the bouncer chair, but I was also able to take my shower. He and I were both comfortable with this routine for many months. Most of the time, he was content or asleep in the bouncer chair. If he cried, I was not concerned because I knew he was in a safe, secure place, and I could monitor him. As my baby grew older, I transitioned to using a play mat and a playpen in my bathroom/bedroom area. By doing this, I was able to keep "shower" on my daily to-do list and know that it would actually happen every day.

After you have created your to-do list and established a schedule to help you achieve your goals, make sure you cross off the items on your list every day. It will make you feel good to see what you can accomplish as a new mother functioning on minimal sleep. Make a new list each day and adjust your routine accordingly if your tasks require additional time or steps. Your baby's needs will change monthly, and sometimes weekly, but if you are accustomed to having a to-do list and a routine that supports you in achieving your tasks, you will adapt to these changes. Having a routine will help you and your baby anticipate what will happen next in your day.

PLAN AND PREPARE

How can you keep yourself accountable and make it easier to accomplish your tasks? The answer is to plan and prepare ahead of time. Since exercise was always a priority on my to-do list, I knew that I had to plan and prepare to have my exercise time. Usually, the only way for me to accomplish this goal was to exercise with my baby in the stroller or carrier. When I woke in the morning, I decided when I wanted to exercise that day. Sometimes, when the baby woke from his mid-morning nap, I fed him right away, changed him, and put him in the stroller for a walk. If I wanted to exercise earlier in the morning, I put my son in the stroller for his first morning nap after he had been fed and changed. Every day, we went for a long walk or run, which was invigorating for me, mentally and physically, and helped me achieve a goal that was important to me. This became part of our daily routine.

Putting in a few minutes of preparation will pay off in the long run and make it easier for you to follow the routine you have created when you have limited windows of time to accomplish your tasks. Preparation and planning were helpful for two reasons. First, I was ready to exercise when my baby was ready instead of running around at the last minute, gathering items, changing clothing, and doing other last-minute tasks. I knew that if I missed my window, my exercise time would not happen. Second, I had time to deal with any unexpected events that occurred, such as a messy diaper explosion, projectile spit-up, or the baby needing a change of clothing.

Here is an example of how it worked for me. Planning and preparing meant that while my baby napped or while he was content, I needed to do several things. I would change into my exercise clothes, use the bathroom, fill my water bottle, and make sure any necessities for the baby were in the stroller. When my son woke from his nap, I was dressed in my running clothes and had everything I needed already in the stroller. Since I usually took the stroller to exercise, I needed to check the air in the stroller tires on a weekly basis. These are all simple tasks, but they are accomplished much more quickly when the baby is asleep or content. Trying to do all these things when the baby was fussy or needed my attention left me feeling flustered and stressed. To make it easier for me to get out the door, I always kept baby supply stashes (i.e., diapers, wipes, etc.) in several key places. Since I always had an extra baby supply stash in my stroller (see

Chapter 3 for more detail), I was prepared and could leave whenever my baby was ready. Further, I was prepared for diaper changes and spit-up that might occur during our time away from home.

If you have been keeping track of your baby's feeding and sleeping times, this information will help you develop a daily schedule so you can plan and prepare for each day. For example, if you want to have time to accomplish certain tasks on your to-do list, and you notice that your baby's longest nap is generally around the same time every day, use that window of time to plan and prepare for the tasks at the top of your to-do list. Of course, babies are human, and naps will vary, but babies also tend to develop consistent patterns. If you have not tried keeping a log of nap and feeding times, it is never too late to start. Logging your baby's feeding and sleeping times will also give you a better understanding of your baby's daily needs, which is discussed further in Chapters 4 and 6.

As a parent, you are responsible for all your baby's basic needs, but do not forget that your own needs are also important. Of course, there were times when it took longer to feed my son, or he spit up, so our walks were shorter on those days. Some days he did not nap in the stroller, or he was fussy, but neither stopped me from getting outside for a walk. Exercise was one of the things on my to-do list that I wanted to accomplish, and I wanted to find a way to make it happen. Generally, my baby calmed down the longer we walked, and if he did not, it made me walk or run faster to get back home. Even when I was tired or frustrated, I reminded myself that I needed this exercise for my own emotional and physical well-being. If you include a few things on your to-do list that you want to accomplish for yourself, it will improve your own emotional state and help you be a better mom.

3

ORGANIZATION

You may feel overwhelmed by the mere thought of trying to get organized with a new baby. It can be challenging to adjust to taking care of someone else in addition to yourself. Despite what you may think, getting organized does not have to be overwhelming. Having simple and effective systems in your life to help you with your daily routine can relieve some of your stress and frustration.

Being "organized" does not necessarily mean your home is tidy and everything is in order. Organized can simply mean being prepared for your daily responsibilities and goals. In the two weeks after I had my first baby, I felt as if I was always running around trying to find the supplies I needed. I knew I had to organize my home to make it easier to care for my baby. I wanted to find ways to meet my baby's needs more efficiently and effectively. You may have a beautiful room or space for your baby, complete with a changing table and crib and decked out with all the latest supplies. You will use that space often, especially before and after naps and perhaps during night feedings. However, after the first couple of weeks, you may find, as I did, that you are changing your baby's diaper in many places other than the baby's room and that you need extra clothes or burp cloths when you are away from home, outside your house, or a staircase away from your essentials. I wanted to have supplies when I needed them and where I needed them. That's where organization comes in to make your life simpler.

One easy way to simplify your life with a newborn is to create a baby supply stash. What is a baby supply stash? Basically, it is your baby's travel bag of necessities. It is a simple process to create baby supply stashes in the places you access the most. Similar to having a travel bag or gym bag, having these supplies readily accessible will make your life easier and less overwhelming. Think of the areas inside and outside your home that you use most frequently with your baby. For me, this was the kitchen, the stroller, my bedroom, and my car. Creating a baby supply stash in each of your most visited places will help reduce chaos and stress in your daily routine. Instead of searching for the pacifier when you are on a walk with your baby or frantically trying to find wipes or anything to absorb liquid when your baby spits up in the car, you will have the supplies you need with you. You and your baby do not want to be out of the house without a fresh diaper or change of clothes when she has a diaper overflow or a massive spit-up. Your baby will be wet and uncomfortable (and probably fussy), and you will feel frustrated and stressed. Your baby supply stash will be a simple way to help you deal with unexpected situations. Although babies can be highly unpredictable, you can get ahead of their game and prepare yourself for most situations.

If your baby has reflux or tends to spit up a lot, keeping extra cloth diapers or old rags and baby bibs in multiple locations of your home, especially in the areas where you typically feed your baby, will make your life easier. My first baby would often spit up midway through nursing and again within thirty minutes of feeding him. I ended up keeping an old rag or cloth diaper on my shoulder throughout the day during the first few months because my son spit up so much. To prevent constantly changing both of our clothes and cleaning the upholstery on the couch, I learned to keep a big basket of cloth diapers and bibs next to the couch where I often nursed him during the day and next to the rocking chair where I nursed him at night. My son wore a bib most days during the first two months, since it was easier to quickly change his bib after a spit-up instead of all his clothing. Preparing yourself for messy cleanups by strategically stashing baby supplies will make your day less stressful.

For someone so small, a baby requires an amazing amount of gear and supplies! However, there is only a handful of supplies you truly need in order to care for your baby when you are away from your main hub. To put together a baby supply stash, first make a short list of the primary supplies you need on a daily basis. To help you get started, here is a preliminary list of my own recommendations. These are merely suggestions, so always consider your daily routine and your baby's needs when creating your own baby supply stashes.

1. Diapers
2. Wipes
3. Burp cloth(s) or small towel(s)
4. Pacifier and pacifier clip
5. Diaper rash cream
6. Old towel or fold-up changing pad
7. Change of clothing
8. Ziploc or plastic bag for dirty diapers and wipes

Once you have collected your baby supplies, put all these items in a small bag you can easily transport. You may need two or three stashes depending on your daily routine and how many locations you want to include, but it is worth it when you are prepared for a diaper blowout or soaked onesie when you are at the store or on a walk. Once you have your baby supply stashes in place, you will feel more organized and prepared for outings with your baby. Having baby supply stashes will take the element of surprise out of many daily situations while away from home (i.e., dropped pacifier, leaky diaper, projectile spit-up, soiled clothing).

The key to making this organizational tool work for you is to replenish the items in your baby supply stashes after you use them. When I bought a new package of diapers, I put most of the diapers near the changing table and always left a few out to put in my various stashes (the car, downstairs, and the stroller). Trust me, you do not want to be in the situation where you are changing your baby's diaper and you realize there are not any clean diapers in your supply stash. I found it helpful to replace supplies as soon as possible after I used them. For example, if I needed to use the extra change of clothing when we were on a walk, I made a point to bring the soiled clothing inside when we returned home so I would remember to put a clean outfit back in the stroller baby supply stash.

One way to make sure your stashes are always well stocked is to keep a running list of the baby items that need replenishing or reordering on your phone or pad of paper. At the end of the week, check your list and see if anything needs to be purchased or if any of your supply stashes need to be restocked. Once you get in the habit of using your stashes, you will not want to be left without any supplies when you need them. Keeping a list of the baby items you use on a regular basis will help your household function more efficiently. No one wants to run out to the store at midnight to purchase a package of diapers!

Implementing some basic organizational systems in your life can help you keep a routine and make it easier to accomplish what you want to do each day. Creating and maintaining your baby supply stashes is one simple way to help you stay organized as a busy mom.

4

UNDERSTANDING YOUR BABY'S FEEDING ROUTINE

Keeping a log of your baby's feeding times helps you create a schedule by predicting when your baby usually gets hungry. Even when your baby is only three weeks of age, you will begin to notice her feeding patterns if you are logging her feeding times. Keep in mind that your baby's feeding schedule changes according to her development and may change monthly, sometimes even weekly, but you will have a better understanding of your baby's daily feeding patterns with each passing week. In the first few weeks, your baby may take a feeding every two to three hours. Each feeding can range from ten to forty-five minutes depending on how quickly your baby nurses or takes her bottle. Fortunately, most babies will become more efficient at feeding as the weeks progress.

My first son was a slow nurser, so I tried to feed him as much as possible each time. By encouraging your baby to have a full feeding, you will help her last for longer stretches before getting hungry again. Yes, it can take a little longer to do each feeding, but the benefit is that your baby will usually sleep longer afterward, which in turn gives you more rest in between feedings. This is especially helpful at night when you want to sleep more than ninety minutes at a time.

During the day, babies will benefit from some awake time following their feeding if you can keep their attention and encourage them to stay alert for a little while to play and interact with them. Babies tend to sleep longer and are better rested if they are awake longer after each feeding. In the first few weeks, babies often need a nap only twenty or thirty minutes following a feeding. With each passing week (and the weeks do pass quickly the older your baby gets!), your baby will stay awake longer and interact more with you.

Following a schedule and routine has always helped me function better, even before having children. When I plan ahead and have a routine, I experience less stress and have more control over my life. With my first child, I wrote down the start time of every single feeding for eight weeks. I admit that may have been excessive, but it did help me plan and organize my days. When I had my second child, I dialed it back a bit and only needed to make a brief list of daily feeding times for a couple of weeks.

Keeping track of your baby's feedings may seem like it would require too much work. You may be wondering how you can fit one more thing into your day. In reality, it requires very minimal time and effort to log your baby's feedings for a few weeks. I thought I could remember what time my baby's last feeding was. I was wrong. When you are only sleeping a few hours each night, all the days and times begin to run together. I found that I could not remember whether I had last fed my baby two hours ago or four hours ago! I thought I had a great memory before having children, but sleep deficiency can affect your recollection of even the simplest things more than you realize.

In the beginning, writing down my baby's feeding times gave me an understanding of his schedule, and after a while, it just became routine. I am not suggesting that you do what I did for eight weeks straight, but it is helpful to start logging feeding times when your baby is between three to four weeks of age so that you have an idea of her needs and feeding schedule.

As a new parent, it can be surprisingly difficult to know when your baby is truly hungry. Generally, babies tend to cry when they are hungry. For most new parents, this is our cue to feed them. Problem: baby cries. Solution: feed the baby. However, this solution does not always work because babies cry for a multitude of other reasons. I could write another book just about the reasons why babies cry. For example, they might be cold. They might be warm. The air might be too dry. They might have a wet diaper. They may need to be burped. They might have indigestion. There may be too much noise. It may be too quiet. The baby's clothing might be uncomfortable. The baby's swaddle might have come undone. The swaddle might be too restrictive. The pacifier may have fallen out of your baby's mouth. The list goes on.

My point is that when your baby cries, it does not necessarily mean she is hungry. In general, if your newborn has a good, full feeding, she should be able to wait two to four hours (give or take) until her next feeding. If she cries within sixty to ninety minutes after a good feeding, consider whether this cry may just be discomfort, restlessness, or one of the many other reasons that a baby could cry. As your baby grows, you will have a better grasp of her hunger cues, but in the beginning, logging your baby's feeding times can help you know when she is truly hungry or if she is crying for some other reason.

Unless you have a log of your baby's feeding times, it's easy to react to crying with the breast or bottle without stopping to think what is actually causing the crying. In my opinion however, giving a baby milk anytime she cries does not create a happy baby. Babies who feed on and off every hour or two do not get a full feeding and tend to expect to be fed on demand. This routine is not sustainable for you or your baby. Feeding on demand can lead to a fussier, overtired baby because she never gets a longer stretch of sleep due to the frequent feedings. In addition, you may find that there is less time to interact and play with your baby due to her fussiness and the frequency of breastfeeding or bottle-feeding. You will also be more tired if you are feeding your baby anytime she cries and may find yourself with minimal time to accomplish anything else during the day. Keeping track of your baby's feeding times can help you understand her needs and determine the best response to her cries. For example, if you just fed your baby ninety minutes ago and she is crying, you could try rocking her, singing to her, giving her a pacifier, taking her outside, or any other number of things to calm her rather than to just feed her.

There are a few ways to encourage your baby to take a full feeding instead of a quick snack so she is full and can go longer stretches between feedings. Since newborn babies often get drowsy during a feeding, you can gently wake your baby by rubbing or tickling her feet or hands or even putting a damp cloth on her feet or forehead. This may stir your baby just enough so that she continues feeding. If your baby is still swaddled or in warm clothing for her feeding, you can unwrap the swaddle or take a layer of clothing off your baby, which may help focus her attention back on nursing or her bottle. You can even change her diaper, which is likely to wake her enough to bring her focus back to feeding.

Keeping track of feeding times does not mean you have to create a detailed account of your baby's feedings each day. Remember, logging feeding times is intended to make your life easier, not more complicated. With my first baby, I simply wrote down the date and times he fed each day on a pad of paper. If you do this for a few weeks, you will have a better understanding of your baby's sleep and feeding patterns and be able to incorporate her feedings into your daily schedule. There are also many apps available for your phone or device to keep track of your baby's feedings, which makes it easier and faster for you to keep track of feeding times. There are even printable feeding charts available online if you prefer that format. Keep in mind that logging your baby's feedings occupies a short window of time in your life. As a mother of four children, I welcome opportunities to help organize and simplify my life. Keeping track of my baby's feeding times was one way for me to do just that.

Keeping a log of feeding times when your baby is a newborn is particularly helpful when you have another caregiver helping with your baby. If a family member or other caregiver gives your baby a bottle, it will be easier for them to care for your baby if they know your baby's approximate schedule for feeding and sleeping. By the time my son was four weeks old, I knew, based on my feeding logs, that he was going to feed at these approximate intervals: 3:00 a.m., 7:30 a.m., 10:00 a.m., 1:00 p.m., 4:00 p.m., 6:30 p.m., 8:30 p.m., and a late-night feeding around 11:00 or 12:00 p.m. Knowing that my baby was generally on the same schedule each day made me feel less anxious. The predictability helped me feel more confident about someone else giving my baby a bottle. If we were on a walk or away from the house, I knew my baby's general schedule, and I would try to be home, or in a place where I could feed him, around those approximate feeding times.

Of course, every day is different, and the exact feeding times vary slightly each day, but the greater understanding you have of your baby's needs will make it easier to create a routine that works for both of you.

THE DREAM FEED

The term "dream feed" was coined by Tracy Hogg, author of Secrets of the Baby Whisperer.[1] The dream feed involves nursing or giving your baby a bottle late at night when she is already asleep. Generally, this will occur anytime between 10:00 p.m. and midnight after your baby has fallen asleep for the night. Most newborns will wake for hunger during the night multiple times, and including a dream feed in your daily routine is intended to decrease the number of times that your baby wakes to feed during the night. The goal of the dream feed is to give your baby an extra feeding to enable her to sleep for a longer stretch at night without waking up hungry again, which in turn helps you to sleep longer too. It works. If your spouse or partner (or family member, babysitter) can stay up and do this late-night feeding, you can even go to bed earlier and catch a few additional hours of sleep.

Details about baby feeding schedules for breastfeeding versus bottle-feeding could fill an entirely separate book. However, I feel it is important to address the dream feed because I think it is an essential element in creating a routine for your baby. Including a dream feed in your daily routine can help your baby develop longer stretches of nighttime sleep. I loved the dream feed because it helped my baby establish consistent sleep patterns and gave me a longer period of sleep between nursing sessions. If you tend to stay up later, or if your spouse or partner is willing to stay up to do the dream feed, I highly recommend that you include a dream feed in your daily routine.

A dream feed is precisely that. Your goal is to feed your baby without disrupting his sleep. *Do everything possible to avoid waking your baby.* Do not turn on the lights. As carefully as you can, lift your baby out of her bed, feed her, and put her right back to bed. Of course, it is always important to make sure to burp your baby before putting her back down, otherwise you may end up with a crib full of spit-up milk. Take care to do everything as quietly as possible without disturbing your baby. Most babies will actually stay asleep throughout this process, and if they wake, they will quickly go back to sleep. We used the dream feed in our daily routine with all four of our children, and I believe it was the primary reason that each of them slept for a longer stretch at night. Your baby's belly will be full, with minimal or no disruption to her sleep, and she will grow accustomed to sleeping longer at nighttime. Your baby's longer stretches of sleep will allow you to achieve a longer, more quality sleep.

Here is an example of how the dream feed can work. I would go to bed between 9:00 p.m. and 10:00 p.m. after my baby went down for his last nap. My husband would do the dream feed around 11:00 p.m. Our son would usually sleep for several more hours after the dream feed until 2:00 a.m. or 3:00 a.m., enabling me to get a good five-hour stretch of sleep between feedings. We had this system down like clockwork. If you are a nursing mother, and you are at ease with someone else giving your baby a bottle of your expressed milk, consider pumping before you go to bed to allow your baby to have a fresh bottle for the dream feed. In addition, pumping may help you feel more physically comfortable at night in the event your baby has a longer stretch of sleep. On nights when my husband could not do the dream feed, I would still go to bed early and get up to nurse for the dream feed. Even though I was getting a shorter continuous stretch of sleep between 10:00 p.m. and 3:00 a.m., I was still sleeping more hours in total, and my baby was developing the sleep habits that would serve all of us well for months and years to come.

5

MAKING YOUR DAILY ROUTINE EASIER WITH STROLLERS AND BABY CARRIERS

Before I had children, I viewed strollers and baby carriers simply as ways to get your baby from one place to another. A means to an end. However, once I became a mom, I discovered that strollers and carriers can also make your life easier by enabling you to accomplish more in your daily routine, keep your hands free, and carve out some time for yourself. With numerous styles and models to choose from, you can find a stroller and baby carrier that work for you.

STROLLERS

When I had my first son, the stroller was my escape from the house. My single jogging stroller, manufactured by BOB Gear and which I would recommend highly, was one of the best baby gifts I received. I used it every single day, rain or shine, sometimes multiple times a day. It enabled me to get out of the house while getting much-needed exercise. I was fortunate that my son loved to nap in the stroller, and even when he did not actually sleep, he loved the fresh air and stimulation of being in a new environment outside. For me, it was a mental and physical escape from the seemingly never-ending routine of feeding, burping, changing, pumping, napping, repeat.

As much as you may love holding your baby, every mom needs a break. Your arms and back need a rest, and using the stroller allows you to be mobile with your baby without carrying her. If your baby will nap in the stroller, use this to your advantage. You can get out of the house for a refreshing break, and your baby can sleep. Babies take so many naps in their first three months, and allowing your baby to nap in the stroller once a day will not jeopardize the nap time routine you have created. In fact, you can make it part of your daily schedule, so that one of your baby's naps is routinely in the stroller in the first few months. As your baby grows, and naps less frequently, she can enjoy awake time in the stroller.

You can run or walk at your own pace with your baby in the stroller. Explore your neighborhood, find trails, or head over to one of the local schools and walk on the track. Many city, county, and state parks have great walking paths or trails as well as playground equipment that your baby will use as she grows. Using the stroller can also enable you to run a few errands, such as mailing a letter, getting coffee, or picking up a few items from the store if you are within walking distance from such places. I used the stroller as much as I could, since it always seemed easier to me than getting my baby in and out of the car seat.

When I had my second son, I used a double stroller, which was not as easy if he was trying to nap, since my toddler's primary goal was to try and wake up his baby brother. Still, the boys enjoyed being near each other most of the time, and I was still able to get outside, exercise, and have a break from the house. Eventually, my toddler rode his scooter while I pushed my baby in the stroller. This allowed the baby to sleep without being interrupted by his brother and helped all of us get outside for fresh air and exercise. I genuinely believe that my children's love of the outdoors began when they were babies. They have been used to outdoor activity almost every day since they were born, and they still prefer outside playtime to anything indoors.

Do not let the rain or cold weather stop you from getting outside. Put on a raincoat or warm clothing and go. There are rain covers designed for many of the popular strollers on the market, or you can use a swaddle blanket to drape over the front to prevent rain and wind from coming into the stroller. Strollers with storage pockets or compartments are particularly useful for your baby supply stash, water bottle, snacks, phone, and other necessities. You can also purchase various attachments for strollers that have a water bottle holder and storage compartments that simply secure to your stroller with ties or Velcro.

Depending upon the brand and model, some strollers can be expensive. If you are not in a position to buy a new stroller, consider borrowing one from a friend or neighbor whose children have outgrown their stroller. Many people still have gently used strollers in great condition sitting in their garages. You can find quality used strollers on local sites such as Nextdoor, Craigslist, and eBay or by visiting a few consignment stores in your area. Most consignment stores for children are very selective about the items they accept for resale. As a result, the strollers you find at a consignment store are usually clean and in great condition for much less than what they would cost new.

BABY CARRIERS

Most new parents find themselves wanting an extra set of hands. Although help may not always be readily available, using a baby carrier allows you to be hands-free while still holding your baby. It is easy to wear your baby in a carrier, especially when she is a newborn. In the newborn months, babies nap often, and keeping them cozy near your body is an excellent way to bond with your baby and keep her warm and happy. Using a baby carrier also gives your arms a rest from holding your baby and keeps your hands free to do other tasks. For many fussy babies, sitting in a carrier or sling is calming and recreates the feeling of being in the womb by keeping them tightly wrapped, warm and secure.

I found that using a carrier is particularly helpful when you want to go to the store with your baby. It is nearly impossible to push a stroller while pushing a shopping cart. Putting your baby in a carrier is also much easier than trying to transfer the infant car seat from the car into the shopping cart. Make your life easier by putting your infant into a carrier or sling and walk into the store without lugging a stroller or car seat. Plus, you have your hands free to do your shopping.

Since most baby carriers are adjustable, many moms are even able to nurse their babies while holding them in the baby carrier. I was never quite coordinated enough to pull this off seamlessly, but I know many moms who did. I was always impressed by the moms who nursed their babies in a carrier or sling because it was quick and convenient. If you use an Ergobaby carrier, there are excellent instructions and tips for breastfeeding your baby in a carrier on the official website.

Using a baby carrier is a simple way to get outside for a walk or hike with your baby. Even in bad weather, you can bundle up or put on a raincoat and lightly drape a swaddle blanket over the top of the carrier to protect the baby's head from getting wet. I often joined other moms in my area on hikes with our infant children. Doing this made our daily routine easier, since we were able to get outdoors, enjoy adult conversation, and exercise while our babies were asleep or content in their carriers.

Babybjörn, Ergo, and Beco are just a few baby carriers on the market that I used and recommend. However, there are so many great products now, and everyone has their own preference for what works best for their lifestyle. Personally, I love the Ergo because I feel it provides the most support, and it has an infant insert that allows it to be used for newborns. I also love the Beco carriers because they enable you to carry your baby on your back or front, and your baby can face in or out. There are numerous baby slings and other types of carriers that you can use in different ways. For example, the Moby Wrap is another type of carrier that is comfortable, soft, washable, and versatile with many different options on how to wear it.

Keep in mind, as with strollers, you do not have to buy a new carrier or sling. Since most carriers are washable, buying a used one is a great option because most parents only use them during the first year. Although you can continue to use a baby carrier for your growing toddler, it becomes more difficult to carry your child for long periods of time due to the increased weight and your child's desire to walk on her own. Nextdoor, Craigslist, eBay, and consignment stores are also reliable sources for finding quality baby gear at a low price. Ask around and see if family, friends, or other moms who have older children would be willing to let you borrow one of their baby carriers. I was happy to pass mine along to friends who had babies after I did. You will find that most moms are willing to share and lend baby items to other parents.

Each baby carrier is different, but all provide useful ways to carry your baby while allowing you to remain hands-free. This was a lifesaver for me. Most babies are content napping in a baby carrier or sling when they are under eight weeks of age. It can take five to ten minutes of walking around, bouncing, or rocking to lull your baby to sleep in the carrier or sling, but once your baby is sleeping, you have the freedom to do other things. You are still able to hold your baby and be close to her, but you can use your hands to make a phone call, check email, fold laundry, eat, or read.

I would be withholding useful information from you if I did not share another benefit of baby carriers. I discovered that even when my baby was in the sling or the baby carrier, I was able to use the bathroom, which was a huge relief. When you are holding your baby in your arms and she falls asleep, you do not have this option unless you put her down and risk waking her up. Since you do not want your precious bundle of joy to wake up from her much-needed nap while snug in the carrier or sling, it is helpful to know that you can take care of your personal needs without disturbing your baby. This may not be possible with every style and type of carrier, but I found it to work well when I was carrying my baby in the Moby Wrap or the Ergo carrier. Slightly loosening the waist strap on your carrier and moving it up higher, and even squatting above the toilet seat, will make it easier to use the bathroom while wearing your baby in a sling or carrier.

As a mom who has navigated the newborn phase four times, I assure you that a baby carrier is one of the most useful and helpful baby gear items you can have. Carriers are a simple way to accomplish more each day while keeping your baby close to you, and you can use carriers well beyond the newborn months. Once my children were between twelve and twenty-four months, I even carried them in the baby carrier on my back while hiking. I encourage you to find a baby carrier that works for you and start making your daily routine easier with your baby.

PART 2: YOUR BABY'S SLEEP

"There was never a child so lovely but his mother was glad to get him to sleep."

— RALPH WALDO EMERSON

I am fortunate that I have four children who are all good sleepers. Did I just get lucky? Maybe. However, I believe that establishing a solid routine for each of my children when they were babies created the foundation for their good sleep habits as toddlers and beyond. My first son slept through the night at six weeks old. My other children all slept through the night between nine and twelve weeks of age. They were all on consistent nap schedules by four weeks of age. As they grew older, my children's routines evolved, but we prioritized the bedtime routine. As a result, my children still find comfort in their nightly bedtime routine and feel secure falling asleep in their own beds at night. Right now, you may be thinking that this is impossible and unrealistic. It is not. It took some planning and work for this to happen, but it was well worth it. When you create an environment and routine that supports consistent sleep patterns, you help your children establish good sleep routines that they will use into child-hood and adulthood.

6

LOGGING YOUR BABY'S SLEEP PATTERNS

Newborn sleep varies widely, but most newborns tend to sleep anywhere from fourteen to eighteen hours in every twenty-four-hour period. From an adult's perspective, that might seem like a lot of sleep, but most newborns are unable to sleep longer than three- to four-hour stretches without feeding. The duration of a daytime nap may be similar to that of a nighttime stretch of sleep when babies are newborns. As babies approach three months of age, the number of hours spent sleeping at night should increase, and the number of hours spent sleeping during the day should decrease. Your baby will be able to stay awake for longer stretches of time during the day and interact with you more. In addition, your baby will begin to sleep for longer stretches of time at night. Nighttime sleep can range from six to eight hours and will increase to ten to twelve hours when your baby is closer to six months of age.

Similar to keeping a feeding log, keeping a short log of when your baby naps will help you determine your baby's sleep patterns. This is helpful for two reasons. One, it gives you a general idea of your daily schedule. This helps you have more control over your time and what you can accomplish each day. Second, it allows you to find time to rest and sleep, which is essential for parents of newborns (and toddlers too!).

I simply kept a pad of paper on the counter and jotted down my baby's nap times for a few weeks. With my second son, I used an app on my phone to track his nap and sleep times. Similar to those for logging feeding times, there are numerous apps that make it simple and quick to keep track of your baby's sleep. After a few weeks, I could already recognize my baby's sleep patterns, and I did not need to record nap times anymore. Although it is not necessary to log sleep times, doing so can help you to understand your baby's sleep patterns and enable you to plan your days. Your baby changes rapidly every week. His sleep schedule will vary monthly, and sometimes even weekly, and understanding your baby's changing sleep patterns can help you adjust to each new phase of his life.

It may seem like more work to make a log of your baby's sleep times, but remember that this requires minimal effort and is *temporary*. Your baby's newborn weeks are such a short part of his life.

7

THE IMPORTANCE OF A SLEEP ROUTINE FOR YOUR BABY

I admit it. I am a slave to the nap. I will rearrange things, leave an event early, and change my schedule to accommodate my children's nap time. Does this sound strange? Maybe. Do my children sleep well? Yes!

Nap time is sacred in my house. This is one of the few times where I can have a moment to myself and accomplish things on my to-do list. It can be tempting to just skip your baby's nap or push the nap too late or too early. If you are with friends or family, it creates extra effort to break away so you can get your baby ready for his nap.

However, after having four children, I know this to be true: babies thrive on routine, and as they grow to be toddlers, routine will become even more important in your life. Children (and most adults for that matter) like to know what is happening next. If you establish good nap habits when your baby is young, it will continue to benefit him. As your baby grows, his nap will continue to be a normal part of his everyday routine. Maintaining a solid sleep routine for your baby is also a key element to having a schedule and carving out some time for yourself. Once your baby is on a good nap schedule, he will get tired at nearly the same times every day and fall asleep with less effort on your part. If it sounds too good to be true, it is not. Creating a sleep routine for your baby requires minimal effort and has significant, lasting results for you and your baby.

A good sleep routine will help your baby sleep better. It will also create consistency for your family. Babies crave predictability and feel safer when they know what is coming next. A consistent bedtime routine is one of the best ways you can help your baby sleep better and longer. One research study on infant sleep concluded that having a consistent nightly bedtime routine is beneficial in improving infant sleep as well as maternal mood. In this study, mothers followed a nightly three-step bedtime routine for two weeks. The study found that these children fell asleep faster with a consistent bedtime routine. It also found that the infants' sleep throughout the night improved, because there was a decrease in the number and the duration of their night awakenings.[1]

One of the greatest benefits of having a routine is that it helps teach your baby how to fall asleep on his own and sleep through the night without your constant intervention. Helping your baby learn this skill, as discussed more in Chapter 15, will be a priceless gift to your baby and to yourself.

The first step is to develop a bedtime routine that is manageable for you. Simple enough, right? Second, you need to follow the routine you created. This step is the more challenging of the two. Of course, there will be days when your routine is disrupted. Life happens! However, make a consistent effort to do everything possible to follow your baby's bedtime routine and put your baby back on the schedule that you have created. If you can establish a simple routine that you can follow every day, even when you travel, it will benefit you and your baby for years to come. Consistency is actually quite attainable with a baby, even a newborn, as long as you create a bedtime routine that is manageable for both of you.

To establish a sleep routine for your baby, first consider the times of day when your baby generally naps. For example, if you notice that your baby gets tired or naps around 9:00 or 9:30 a.m. in the morning most days, you may choose to establish 9:00 a.m. as the baby's first morning nap time. Babies and children thrive on routine and often put themselves on their own nap schedules if you watch for their cues. How do you know when your baby is getting tired? There are several telltale signs your baby will give you. Pay attention to these sleep cues. Your baby is likely to yawn multiple times, rub his eyes, become cranky, or have a dazed look in his eyes when he is close to his optimal sleep time. Once you see these signs, your baby is ready for his nap. Waiting too long after seeing your baby's sleep cues will likely result in a short nap or no nap.

For example, if you have established that 9:00 a.m. is generally the time of your baby's first morning nap, do not wait until 9:00 a.m. to begin your baby's pre-nap routine. Around 8:45 a.m., you can prepare for your baby's nap by doing the things that need to be completed *before* your baby takes his nap. This may include changing the baby's diaper, making sure that he is swaddled or has his sleep sack (depending upon the age of your baby), dimming the lights, singing to your baby, reading to your baby, and putting him in his crib for his nap. Again, do not wait until the 9:00 a.m. nap time, when your baby is overtired, to do these things. Prepare and be ready for your baby's nap, and maintain your daily schedule. If you start the process after your baby is already crying and overtired, you may miss your window of time to get your baby down for his nap. Infants (and all children for that matter) can become overstimulated and overtired, which makes it challenging to get them to sleep. Even when this does happen, (and it will), having a sleep routine will make it easier for you to push through the frustration of putting an overtired and overstimulated baby to sleep. Once you have an established routine, your baby will respond to the patterns you have created, and this will help calm him. In addition, by making your baby's nap a priority, you will find that you are more organized and prepared for what you want to accomplish each day.

The same rules of nap time apply to baby's bedtime in the evening. The routine you use during the day for nap should be the same or similar to your routine at night. Your baby will respond to familiarity, and when he knows what to expect, the nighttime process will become more streamlined for you and your baby. With newborns, the first few weeks can be highly unpredictable, but by four to six weeks of age, it is not too early to start developing consistent bedtimes.

As your baby begins sleeping longer stretches at night, it will become even easier to institute consistent bedtimes. If you start developing a routine early on, your baby will begin to recognize the steps in his sleep routine and keep a consistent sleep schedule. When your baby falls asleep at about the same time every night, his body chemistry regulates itself around that consistent time, creating a strong urge to sleep.[2] To establish a strong sleep routine for your baby, make a concerted effort to put your baby to sleep at the same time every night as he approaches three months of age. It is understandable that bedtime might vary by fifteen to twenty minutes, but consistency with time is the overall goal when establishing a solid sleep routine for your baby.

Establishing a consistent pre-sleep routine before each bedtime is fundamental to creating and maintaining an effective sleep schedule. There are several ways to create a reliable bedtime routine for your baby. The simple solutions outlined in the next several chapters will help your baby stay on schedule and have familiarity and predictability in his days and nights.

8

BEDTIME ROUTINE TIP 1:
SINGING TO YOUR BABY

It is never too early to introduce your child to music. One of the things I learned by attending Music Together classes for years with each of my babies was the importance of music in a child's life at an early age. The teachers of these classes always emphasized that babies love the sound of their parent's voice. Regardless of whether you think you can sing or what you think your voice sounds like, your baby will love hearing you sing to him. In the Music Together song-books, there is an excellent discussion about the influence of parents on their child's musical development: "the routine quiet of nap or bed may make the child receptive to your singing the lullabies or songs, so put aside your own opinion of your voice for a moment and sing to your young child with the sweetest voice she knows."[1] In addition, singing to your baby exposes him to different words, tones, and sounds and helps him to understand words and body language long before he is even able to speak his native tongue.

Your child loves the sound of you singing to him. It is soothing and comforting to him. Singing to your baby is a universal expression of your love for your child and a way to bond with your baby. One study of the relationship between music and infants concluded that mothers who sing lullabies to their infants can improve maternal-infant bonding. This study also found that singing to infants can reduce crying and can have a positive effect on maternal stress.[2] Research performed on the connection between mothers and infants through song has found that infants are able to process music and engage with the person singing. Further, mothers also benefit from singing to their babies, since it can provide distraction from negative emotions and thoughts and help a mother feel empowered as a parent.[3]

As mentioned earlier, babies thrive on predictability and routine, so including singing in your bedtime routine will help ease the transition from awake time to sleep time. Finding a few songs that seem to calm your baby can help you create a strong pre-sleep routine. Your baby will look forward to those songs that he recognizes and associate the songs with sleep time. Singing familiar songs to your baby may be more beneficial to calming your baby and mitigating infant distress, since familiar songs can evoke pleasure.[4]

Research involving the relationship between music and preterm babies has produced interesting results also. One study concluded that soothing sounds, such as singing lullabies, can calm preterm babies and their parents. The lullabies even improved the infants' sleeping and eating patterns and decreased the parents' stress levels.[5]

Infants are unable to self-regulate and express themselves through language and in other ways that adults can. Self-regulation is "the ability to manage one's emotions, physical needs, and arousal. Babies need adults who can help them learn this skill of self-regulation."[6] If singing to your child calms him, you are communicating with your baby by showing him that you hear his frustration and are singing to help him calm down. Your baby may stop crying when you sing, or he may reach for you or look at you intensely. These responses are your baby's way of communicating with you and letting you know that the music is soothing to him and helping him calm down.

Singing to your baby is easy to incorporate into your baby's bedtime routine. You do not need a Grammy-winning voice or any special musical talents. A simple version of "Twinkle, Twinkle, Little Star" is always a hit with most children. One of the great things about singing to your baby is that you can pick the songs. Make up your own songs or sing classic lullabies, nursery rhymes, or some of your old favorites. The bottom line is that you are in charge of the song selection, so sing what you like and what your baby responds to best. Your baby will grow accustomed to hearing a song before bedtime, and this routine will help him relax and prepare for sleep.

9

BEDTIME ROUTINE TIP 2:
READING TO YOUR BABY

Reading to your baby is something you can easily incorporate into your nightly bedtime routine. It can help relax and calm your baby before sleep, especially when he is fussy or upset. Reading to your baby can also distract him from whatever might be frustrating him and place the focus on something he can see, touch, and hear. Besides being a great addition to the bedtime routine, reading to your baby will benefit him far beyond the newborn months. Reading to your child as an infant provides a solid foundation for a lifetime of literacy. In addition, the special time you spend reading to your baby strengthens the bond between you.

According to the National Education Association, it is never too soon to start reading to your child. A child who learns to associate reading with enjoyment is more likely to read for pleasure as an adult. You can help create your child's love for books when your child is still a baby. I began reading to my children every day when they were infants. We read before every nap and bedtime, and throughout the day as well. My older children have become independent readers and still read before bedtime. In fact, they use reading as a method for calming down and regulating their emotions.

Reading before your baby's nap time and bedtime can become a part of your sleep routine. Your baby loves the sound of your voice, but not just when you are singing; infants even love to hear words read from a book. Even though your baby may not understand everything you are reading, he is hearing your voice and listening to different tones and sounds. Reading creates a calming atmosphere before sleeping, and your baby will look forward to hearing your voice and will associate it with nap time. Creating sleep cues, such as reading, also makes it easier for your baby to make the transition from awake to asleep. Pediatrician Dr. Sarah Klein lists the many benefits of reading, one of which is establishing routines.[1] According to Dr. Klein, children thrive on routine, and reading can be a great addition to your daily bedtime routine. If you get in the habit of reading before bed, a book can signal to your baby that it is time to slow down and get ready for sleep.

In addition to being a beneficial step in your baby's bedtime routine, reading aloud to infants improves their early literacy skills. One recent study suggests that reading to infants and toddlers has a lasting effect on their language, literacy, and early reading skills.[2] In addition, the American Academy of Pediatrics recommends that parents begin reading aloud to their children in infancy to encourage word learning, literacy, and positive family relationships. Dr. Klein also explains that early reading can provide the foundation for language as well as tools for forming social and emotional skills. Creating a reading routine with your baby can be the first step of your child's appreciation of books. By reading to your child daily, you are teaching him that reading is important to your family. You are modeling a positive behavior for your child and effortlessly supporting his literacy skills every time that you read to him.

Reading to your baby creates a special bond between you. Babies are comforted by the sound of their parent's voice while being rocked or held. Almost any child, whether he is a baby or a toddler or elementary school age, loves the special attention he receives when someone reads to him. Children look forward to hearing a story, whether it is something new or a story they have heard fifty times before. Even my oldest children, who are avid, independent readers, still prefer when I read to them each night because reading together provides the special one-on-one time that has been part of their bedtime routine since they were babies.

How do you select appropriate books for your newborn baby? Even though your baby does not speak or read yet, he is always listening to you and watching you. Selecting board books with bright colors, interesting shapes, and different textures is a good place to start with babies. Your baby will be simply observing in his early months, but as he grows, he will begin to recognize shapes and colors and will explore the book by touching and grabbing it, and even putting it in his mouth.

Including a few minutes of reading to your baby before his nap gives both of you special time to cuddle and interact without distraction while calming your baby before he sleeps. Make reading a part of your baby's bedtime routine every day that you can.

10

BEDTIME ROUTINE TIP 3: SWADDLING

To swaddle or not to swaddle? Some parents feel that it is not worth the extra time and effort. Other parents claim that their baby does not like to be swaddled or fusses too much to be swaddled. There are so many benefits of swaddling that I strongly encourage you to give it a try with your baby. Swaddling is worth the minimal time and effort involved for one important reason: *your baby will sleep better when he is swaddled.*

If you have not swaddled a baby or seen a baby swaddled, you are not alone. I was unfamiliar with swaddling until I was in my third trimester and was introduced to the concept of swaddling in a baby care class I took with my husband. I remember thinking that swaddling seemed a little awkward at first, but after two attempts, we quickly figured it out. My husband was coined the Swaddle Master because he perfected the art of swaddling, and our babies could not break out of a Daddy swaddle. I love the pictures of my babies swaddled with their cute little heads poking out of the top of the swaddle blanket.

Swaddling is a simple method of wrapping your baby to keep him warm and secure. When you swaddle a baby, you wrap the entire torso, arms, and legs in a thin blanket and secure it tightly. Yes, it takes a few practice runs to get a tight, snuggly swaddle, but in my opinion, it is worth it. It may take a few tries to get the swaddle routine down. The swaddle may come undone multiple times. Do not be discouraged! Swaddling is quite simple and natural once you get the hang of it.

Some babies will fuss and fight the swaddle initially, but once they are wrapped up and secure, they are usually content and will sleep more soundly. Your baby may fuss or resist because he is overtired. He is probably unable to calm himself on his own, and putting him in a swaddle will help relax your baby and prepare him for sleep.

Keep in mind that swaddling is a short stage in your baby's life. Yes, it may add a minute to your bedtime routine, but it is worth it when your baby sleeps better. Generally, you will only swaddle your baby during the first eight to twelve weeks. After that, most babies can get out of their swaddle and roll to their stomachs, so swaddling is not necessary after that point.

BASICS OF SWADDLING

Swaddling is a technique that parents all over the world have used for thousands of years. Swaddling has many benefits, the most important of which is that it helps babies sleep. This alone should be a good enough reason to swaddle from a new parent's perspective! Dr. Harvey Karp, author of The Happiest Baby on the Block, believes swaddling can have a significant effect on a baby's sleep and explains that "just by swaddling your baby, you may increase his sleeping periods from three to four or even six hours at a stretch."[1]

A study comparing infant sleep habits found that swaddling significantly reduced not only the time an infant spent awake but also the rate of spontaneous awakening, both of which promoted more quiet sleep.[2] Spontaneous awakening occurs because babies often make sudden movements, even when sleeping. A baby's natural reflex to startle and move his body is minimized when the baby is wrapped in a swaddle. Swaddling also protects infants from scratching their faces with their tiny (but powerful) fingers. Even if you keep those little fingernails trimmed, babies are inclined to explore their face with their fingers. When your baby begins to roll around more when he sleeps, he will wake himself up nearly every time he tries to move. Rolling and moving are exciting to watch when babies are awake during the daytime but not in the middle of the night. Babies wake themselves numerous times an hour just by trying to move their arms, legs, or torso. Swaddling keeps your baby in a tight, secure wrap and limits your baby's waking from his own movements. Once a baby can roll to his side or stomach, many parents choose to stop swaddling. Some babies may need to be swaddled longer, but if your baby is sleeping well most nights, you may be comfortable stopping swaddling.

Swaddling recreates the feeling babies had in the womb of being warm, secure, and confined. In his book Healthy Sleep Habits, Happy Child, Dr. Marc Weissbluth explains that "gentle pressure, such as that experienced while embraced or hugged, makes us feel good. Swaddling or gentle wrapping... or being held in a soft baby carrier or sling are other ways to exert gentle pressure... perhaps the sensation of gentle pressure resembles a state of comfort that the baby feels before he is born."[3] Swaddling is particularly helpful for fussy and colicky babies. Since swaddling is similar to the cozy, warm feeling of being in the womb, babies may have less anxiety and stress when swaddled. The feeling of being wrapped and held enables the baby to learn to self-soothe and fall asleep without you having to constantly hold him to provide that same feeling.

Swaddling your baby also helps your baby sleep in a safe position. There is considerable research showing that babies need to be put to sleep on their backs to reduce the risk of sudden infant death syndrome (SIDS).[4] Swaddling prevents the baby from rolling over to his stomach, which is the sleeping position most associated with the occurrence of SIDS. Even when your baby is swaddled, remember to always put your baby to sleep on his back. Dr. Harvey Karp addresses safe sleep habits and explains that babies should sleep alone, on their backs, and in a crib (or similar safe place) for as long as possible. Dr.

Karp also recommends swaddling your baby before sleep because swaddling prevents your baby from getting disturbed by his own sudden movements.[5]

Many babies struggle to fall asleep flat on their backs. This may be attributable to the fact that they were not in the supine position in the womb. One study suggests that swaddling may be a good strategy for parents of infants who have difficulty sleeping in the supine position.[6] When a baby is swaddled, it provides an extra level of comfort and snugness that is not found by placing your baby flat on his back in the crib.

The basic swaddle method is best achieved using a thin receiving blanket or swaddle blanket. There are many blankets on the market now made for the specific purpose of swaddling. To begin, spread out the blanket on a flat surface in a diamond shape. Take the top corner of the diamond and fold it toward you to make a small triangle out of the folded piece. Place the baby's feet at the bottom point of the diamond, closest to you. The baby's head should be just past the folded edge that you created (with his neck right against the fold). Next, take the right side of the diamond you have made with the blanket, stretch this fabric over your baby's chest, and tuck the blanket around his left side and under his back. Continue by folding the bottom part of the blanket up and over baby's feet and legs. The baby's legs should bend slightly at the knee and should not be rigidly straight. Then, take the left side of the diamond and wrap it around and under as much of the baby's body as you can. When doing this, stretch the blanket and wrap it tightly. Secure the remaining diamond corner by tucking it under the folds of the blanket that you have wrapped around the baby. Do not leave out any corners, and make sure it is secured well. As you practice it, you will be able to swaddle more efficiently.

There are a few alternatives to the basic swaddle blanket. Swaddle sleep sacks are a great way to keep your baby warm and snug while also limiting his movements. Some sleep sacks use Velcro tabs; others use fabric panels that tie to secure the sleep sack. These swaddle sleep sacks are easy to use with newborns and foolproof in the middle of the night. The downside to the Velcro sleep sacks is that babies tend to get out of this type of swaddle more easily than swaddle blankets as they get older. Also, make sure to fasten Velcro tabs together when washing to prevent the Velcro from sticking to other clothing items and damaging them.

Another product that I used with all my babies during the first eight weeks and would recommend highly is the Miracle Blanket. This product is made of stretchy cotton that allows you to get a tight, secure swaddle around your baby. It takes a step out of the traditional swaddle process because there is a small built-in pocket which tucks her feet and legs nicely into the swaddle. The stretchy material enables you to get a tight wrap, and the fabric panels are easy to tuck into the main body of the swaddle. The Miracle Blanket requires slightly more effort than simply securing Velcro tabs together, but it works well to keep the baby's limbs securely wrapped, which is what you want, especially in the middle of the night.

VARIATIONS ON SWADDLING

There are a few variations on swaddling, so if you're having trouble, be persistent and try one of the following variations.

Some babies prefer to have one arm out (like my fourth child). After swaddling him for a week, he still seemed restless and frustrated. I noticed that he was moving one side of his body more than the other side, in particular his right arm and hand, so I tried swaddling him as I had before but without including his right arm in the swaddle. After this, he was relaxed and slept much better. Keep in mind that babies will often scratch their faces, so you may want to put a sock or mitten over your baby's hand if you choose to swaddle with one arm out to prevent the baby from scratching his face.

After our second son (a.k.a. Houdini) broke out of his swaddle numerous times, we tried using a double swaddle and succeeded in preventing further magic tricks. To do a double swaddle, we wrapped a thin blanket around our son in a normal swaddling technique. Then, we used another swaddle blanket just around the lower half of his body and legs. Having an extra layer seemed to keep the swaddle secure and tight, and my son slept better. Another option is to use a swaddle sleep sack or Miracle Blanket and do a double swaddle by using a very thin blanket over the sleep sack, which holds everything together nicely.

As babies become more mobile, some babies do well with only their bottom half swaddled and both arms out. To do a half swaddle, place your baby on the triangular folded swaddle blanket with the blanket just under his armpits. Follow the same swaddle wrap described above but wrap and secure it across his chest and back, just under his armpits. I found this approach to be helpful once my baby was using his arms more, around eight to twelve weeks of age, and starting to try to roll over. This approach ensures that your baby stays warm and cozy by having the bottom half of his body wrapped and secure but allowing less movement and less opportunity for the baby to wake himself.

To help your baby sleep better and longer, make swaddling part of your baby's bedtime routine in the first few months. By swaddling before every nap, your baby becomes accustomed to the routine of swaddling. Yes, he may resist it at times, but this also means he is associating swaddling with bedtime. Experiment with different ways of swaddling and see what works best for your baby at different stages. You and your baby will both benefit from the routine of swaddling.

11

BEDTIME ROUTINE TIP 4: USE A PACIFIER

The pacifier is one of the best ways to calm and soothe your baby and give yourself a break. Giving your child a pacifier before bedtime can also be part of your baby's sleep routine. Sucking on a pacifier soothes most babies and allows them to relax. Your baby will likely sleep better and longer, which means you will likely sleep better also.

Pacifiers have numerous benefits. Research has shown that pacifier use during sleep decreases the risk of SIDS.[1] Pacifiers will help your baby calm down when he is upset or frustrated while also providing you with some relief from your baby's crying. Pacifiers can also provide relief for infants during airplane travel when there are air pressure changes during takeoff. They can also serve as a distraction during stressful events, such as doctor visits that involve shots or other tests. In addition, pacifiers enable you, as the mother, to have a break from breastfeeding or bottle-feeding. Often, babies just want to be calmed by the sucking reflex and do not necessarily need another feeding. Pacifiers can provide the same sucking sensation that they receive from nursing or using a bottle without the actual milk. Offering a pacifier after a feeding, or at other times when he is fussy or upset, can calm and relax your baby.

Once your baby understands the sucking reflex and can keep the pacifier in his mouth, there is a good chance he will fall asleep faster and stay asleep longer. The sucking reflex helps babies self-soothe. This is important for a small human being who does not know many ways of calming himself. When used as part of your baby's sleep routine, it can relax and comfort your baby and help him achieve quality sleep.

Some babies take any pacifier without hesitation. Others prefer a certain brand, material, or shape. When choosing a pacifier, select a size based on your baby's age. You may consider having a few different types of pacifiers on hand to determine which kind of pacifier your baby prefers.

When first presented with a pacifier, many babies will spit it out and refuse to suck on it. This is very common, since the pacifier is something new to them, and the shape and texture is different from the breast or bottle. The first time I gave my second son a pacifier, he moved it around in his mouth for a few seconds and spit it out. This happened multiple times. I found it helpful to gently hold the pacifier in his mouth for ten seconds or so until he started sucking on it. I remember holding the pacifier in my newborn son's mouth while he sat in the bouncer chair for what seemed like an eternity, hoping he would suck on that pacifier and fall asleep. In reality, I was just exhausted, and it was merely a few minutes that had passed when I observed that he had fallen asleep, happily sucking on the pacifier.

The benefits of the pacifier are worth the effort to keep trying even if your baby resists the pacifier on your first few attempts. Often, the baby will still spit it out many times. Do not give up. Try using different shapes and brands of pacifiers. Try offering the pacifier at different times of the day (and night) when the baby is *not* hungry. You can also try gently touching the roof of your baby's mouth with the end of the pacifier. A partner, other caregiver, or family member may have the magic touch of introducing your baby to the pacifier. If you are the primary milk or bottle source, your baby might be more willing to accept the pacifier initially from someone else from whom he is not expecting milk.

Another way to encourage your baby to suck on the pacifier is to gently try and pull the pacifier out of his mouth as soon as you notice him starting to suck on the pacifier. Using reverse psychology to convince your baby to take the pacifier can work, since he is likely to want to keep the pacifier in his mouth if you are trying to take it away. Similar to the scenario when you are trying to take a toy away from a toddler or a pet, your baby may resist giving up the pacifier when you attempt to pull it away.[2]

Unless your baby is upset and crying, do not reinsert the pacifier in his mouth once he is sleeping. Let sleeping babies sleep. If your baby spits out the pacifier, he is likely sleeping soundly and does not need the assistance of the pacifier for the duration of his sleep time. In her book <u>The Baby Whisperer Solves All Your Problems</u>, Tracy Hogg explains that most babies who suck on a pacifier to fall asleep will continue to sleep after the pacifier falls out, and "using a pacifier when a baby wakes up early from a nap or during the middle of the night is also a good way to test whether your baby is actually hungry or just needs to suck."[3]

You can save yourself time and money by purchasing a few washable pacifier clips. These clip or tie to your baby's clothing, swaddle blanket, or sleep sack and keep the pacifier from dropping on the floor or getting wedged somewhere in between the crib mattress and the crib and countless other places in your home, car, and stroller. As your baby grows and is able to use his hands more, he will be able to grab the pacifier himself and put it back into his mouth. Pacifier clips are even more useful when taking your baby in the stroller (or anywhere in public) so that the pacifier does not end up on the ground. They are essential for airport travel, since a pacifier on the floor of an airplane may as well go right into the trash. There are also several kinds of cases and holders for pacifiers that zip closed and have a strap to attach to your diaper bag, stroller, or purse. These are helpful to use anytime you leave the house or travel.

Make sure to wash your baby's pacifier with soap and water every day to avoid bacteria developing on the pacifier. Make it simple for yourself by getting in a routine of washing the pacifiers when you wash bottles, pump parts, or other items for your baby.

Often, parents are concerned that using a pacifier will lead to nipple confusion and affect their baby's desire to breastfeed or take a bottle. Some people believe that nipple confusion can occur with breastfed babies when they are given a bottle or pacifier too soon after birth. Since the shape of a pacifier or a bottle nipple differs from the shape of a breast nipple, and the flow of milk is different, some parents and experts believe infants may develop a preference for one type of nipple over another.[4] There are different recommendations on how old your baby should be when you first offer the pacifier to avoid nipple confusion, but most range between two and four weeks of age. Dr. Harvey Karp recommends that it is best to avoid pacifiers until nursing is well established but also notes that research has shown that most babies can suck on a pacifier without experiencing nipple confusion.[5] One study evaluated the use of pacifiers with breastfed infants when infants were fifteen days old. The conclusion of this study was that the introduction of the pacifier had not affected the prevalence or duration of breastfeeding when the infants were evaluated again at three months of age.[6] I breastfed each of my babies for a year and chose to introduce the pacifier when they were between eight and fourteen days old. I found that waiting until they were comfortable breastfeeding without any issues, which will vary with every baby, helped us avoid any problems with nipple confusion.

Other parents hesitate to use a pacifier for fear that they will not be able to wean their baby off the pacifier. Limiting pacifier use and eventually weaning your baby off it are not difficult and well worth every moment that your baby is comforted by using the pacifier. Once your baby approaches six months of age, you can begin by limiting the pacifier to sleep time or certain situations where there can be heightened fussiness, such as getting shots at the doctor or flying on an airplane.

Each of my four children used a pacifier routinely as a newborn. Once they were between six and nine months old, they transitioned to using a pacifier only for sleeping and sometimes during travel or doctor visits. I was able to wean each one of my children from the pacifier completely without any difficulty when they were toddlers. Remember that you, as the parent and caregiver, are in control of pacifier use, and you set the limits for such use. Rest assured; you will be able to wean your child off the pacifier.

Giving your baby a pacifier can help him sleep better and make your life easier. Using pacifiers helps create a calmer environment for everyone in your family. The pacifier is an exceptional sleep aid that helped each of my babies fall asleep on their own and sleep more soundly, which in turn helped our family get more sleep. Give your baby the pacifier. Your baby will be happier. You may find yourself feeling happier too.

12

BEDTIME ROUTINE TIP 5: WHITE NOISE

Parents often complain that their baby cannot stay asleep or is woken up by household or outside noises. When I had my first child, I thought I would have to keep the house silent every time my baby napped. First of all, this is unrealistic. Second, most babies actually are able to sleep well with some noise. Most loud, sudden noises will disturb a baby who is sleeping, but continuous background noise can often lull a baby to sleep or help the baby maintain a sound sleep.

You are already changing so many aspects of your life when you have a new baby. You do not need to reduce all noise in your home every time your baby sleeps. Trying to create a completely quiet home is impossible and stressful! A simple solution is to use white noise in your baby's room. You can use a sound machine designed solely to produce white noise. You can also use a fan, an air purifier, a clock radio set to static, or an app on your device. I have also found bathroom ceiling exhaust fans to be a great source of continuous white noise when we traveled. I would often put my baby's crib or pack and play in the bathroom with the fan turned on the whole night. Whatever form you choose, keep in mind that you will want to use the white noise source for the entire duration of your baby's sleep time.

Babies under six months of age spend about half of their sleep time in active REM, a lighter stage of sleep during which your baby's eyes may move while his eyelids are closed, and he may jerk or twitch his limbs or fingers.[1] During this stage of sleep, your baby may awaken or startle in response to noises that would not typically awaken him during the non-REM stage of sleep.[2] White noise can help mask these outside noises that would normally wake him.

Studies have shown that white noise helps babies fall asleep and stay asleep longer. In one study, 80% of the infants who were exposed to white noise fell asleep in a short time compared to only 25% of infants with no white noise exposure.[3] For parents of newborns, using white noise is an easy and simple way to help their babies sleep. White noise works by blocking out unwanted noise from other rooms and setting a calm, soothing tone for the baby's nap time. White noise reduces the outside stimulation (voices, doorbells, phones, garbage trucks, etc.) that can overwhelm babies and interrupt their sleep or disturb their attempt to fall asleep.

If your baby is sleeping in your room, the white noise may help you sleep better also. For such tiny humans, newborns are surprisingly noisy. They make all kinds of noises while they are sleeping that can disrupt your sleep. White noise will mask some of your baby's grunting and snorting noises, which will help you sleep more soundly.

White noise has also been linked to a reduction in the risk of SIDS. One study concluded that fan use during infant sleep is associated with a seventy-two percent decrease in the risk of SIDS.[4] This may be attributable to the recirculating of air or the white noise emitted by the fan, but the fact that there is an association between white noise and the risk of SIDS is enough justification for most parents to use white noise.

Using a white noise app on your phone or device can be a great option, but if you will need the device at some point during your baby's nap or sleep time, you may want to find an alternative source of white noise. If you do use your phone to provide white noise, make sure to turn it on sleep mode or silence it so your baby is not constantly disturbed by other notifications from your phone. You do not want a loud, jarring "new message" alert to wake your sleeping baby.

If you choose to have a small white noise machine in your baby's room, I recommend buying one that has several settings so you can find a level and sound that works best for your baby. Some white noise machines come in compact sizes to make traveling easier for parents and babies. Most white noise machines plug into a standard outlet. Some sound machines also have backup battery power. Others have the capability to charge and hold a charge for a limited period of time. This comes in handy if your power goes out (which has happened to me countless times). Keep in mind that these sound machines will need to be recharged after use, since they last for a limited number of hours. A few of the newer sound machines can even be paired with an app to enable you to adjust the volume or timer without going into your baby's room.

There are many kinds of white noise sounds. Ultimately, you should use the sound that works best for your baby. However, keep in mind that monotonous, low-pitch, and dull sounds often lull babies to sleep best. In my experience, sounds that are similar to those produced by a fan or hair dryer seem to work best for lulling a baby to sleep, as opposed to ocean waves, birds, nature sounds, or other inconsistent sounds. Try to avoid placing the white noise machine right next to your baby's crib and keep the volume at a medium to low setting.

I cannot say enough about the benefits of white noise. When the power went out at our house, I was more concerned about not having my white noise machine than anything else! I am just kidding... sort of. Once I started using white noise with my baby, his sleep improved. My sleep improved. Now, everyone in our family sleeps more soundly and longer on a consistent basis because I have a small white noise machine in each of our bedrooms. Using white noise is a simple solution that you can use every day as part of your sleep routine to help your baby sleep better.

13

BEDTIME ROUTINE TIP 6: DARK ROOM

As humans, we all have circadian rhythms. Circadian rhythms are mental, physical, and behavioral changes over a twenty-four-hour period that are primarily affected by exposure to light and dark.[1] Circadian rhythms affect many important functions in our bodies, such as temperature regulation, hormone release, eating, and digestion.[2] For newborns, the circadian rhythm takes about eight to ten weeks to develop. Once the infant's body begins to develop a rhythm of cortisol production and melatonin, the infant's sleep cycle will have more regularity. Melatonin is a hormone that your brain produces in response to darkness, and exposure to light at night can block melatonin production.[3] Even though your baby's circadian rhythms may not be fully developed, exposing your baby to regular cues such as darkness during nap time and bedtime and natural light, preferably outdoors, during the day will help your baby develop his sleep cycle.

Once you have created a dark space for your baby to sleep, your baby will associate the darkness with sleep, whether it is his daytime nap or nighttime sleep. Dr. Janet Krone Kennedy explains that as a baby's melatonin is beginning to work for him, it is important for the baby to sleep in a dark room because any light will interfere with his release of melatonin. [4] Kennedy explains further that making it dark for naps and light for awake time creates a contrast that helps the baby's natural biorhythm and predictable sleep to develop. When it is daytime, the light suppresses the release of melatonin and signals to your baby that it is time to wake up. When your baby is awake, make sure you open the curtains or blinds and create a bright place for your baby to engage with you and be stimulated by his environment.

Keeping your baby's room dark for every daytime nap and for night-time sleep should be part of your baby's sleep routine. A bright, light room will create distractions for your baby and make it more difficult for him to sleep. By contrast, a dark room will create a calming atmosphere. Keeping your baby in a dark environment during the day for naps simulates nighttime and improves the chances of your baby sleeping better and longer. My children's rooms resembled dark caves, but I felt that the darkness was essential in creating a good sleep environment for them. My children associated the darkness with nap time, and they slept soundly for long stretches in those rooms. By blocking out the light, your baby will not be distracted by the sun, shadows, toys, pictures, or windows to the outside. During the day, when your baby is awake, is a perfect time to expose him to light, noise, and outdoors. During the night, or during his nap time, is the appropriate time to eliminate the distractions of sights and sounds.

When your baby is a newborn, you will see him several times during the night. Whenever possible, limit the stimulation and light during these nighttime awakenings. For example, keep the lights off or lowered, or use a very dim night-light when entering the room in the middle of the night to feed your baby or to change his diaper. Try to keep the encounters with your baby during the night brief, with minimal noise, light, and stimulation so your baby can return to sleep as quickly and easily as possible. Turning on bright lights and making noise will greatly reduce your chances of getting your baby back to sleep quickly.

To create a dark room, I highly recommend investing in some blackout curtains for your baby's room. Blackout curtains or shades can transform your baby's sleep environment and patterns in a positive way when they are part of your baby's sleep routine. These have been a lifesaver (or napsaver!) for us. There are many reasonably priced, quality blackout curtains in different sizes, patterns, fabrics, and colors that you can easily tack up with a small nail or pushpin on the trim or above the window. Some panels have tabs or pockets which can be fitted on a curtain rod. I prefer to just use pushpins or small nails to tack them up over the frame of the window or sliding door (depending on the windows you have in the baby's room or your bedroom). This option was appealing to me because I could take them down and move them easily. This also comes in handy if the panels need to be washed or if you are moving or changing your child's room. It is easy to tie the panels to the side or pin them up if you prefer to have more light in the room during the day. Many of the panels come with tiebacks for this purpose.

When we traveled, I simply took down a few blackout curtains, folded them, and put them in one of our bags (along with a few pushpins). Dark sheets, towels, or blankets at your destination are a great alternative to the panels if you are tight on packing space. I have used all sorts of fabrics to darken various rooms to help my children sleep better and longer. Another option is to put the baby's crib or pack and play in a bathroom or closet. This may seem odd, but a large closet with a door or a bathroom without windows can create an optimal sleep environment for your baby when you are traveling, especially when there are time zone differences, and it is light during times when your baby is accustomed to sleeping.

Pay attention to other light near your baby's room, such as a bright hallway light or a connecting bathroom light. Keep those lights off or dimmed when your baby is sleeping, since the light can be distracting to your baby.

The simple step of creating a dark space supports your baby's natural circadian rhythm for better sleep. Better sleep for your baby means better sleep for you. In turn, if you are getting better sleep, you can offer your baby more quality time when he is awake.

14

BEDTIME ROUTINE TIP 7:
BEDTIME BATH

Many babies will benefit from a warm bath before going to sleep. You need to bathe your baby anyway, so consider making the bath part of your baby's bedtime or nap time routine. Babies with reflux tend to spit up more than normal, so your baby may need a bath after a few messy feedings. My first baby had reflux and spit up several times a day, every single day, for four months. Even though I changed his clothing multiple times a day, he still had a lingering scent of sour milk. When he was about four weeks old, I started giving him a bath three to four times a week before bedtime to rinse him off and reclaim his sweet baby smell. By doing this, I also discovered that a warm bath calmed him and significantly reduced or eliminated any fussiness and crying, and prepared him for sleep. As a result, I decided to make the bath a permanent part of my son's bedtime routine.

Research has shown that a warm bath before bedtime can help us fall asleep and improve our sleep quality.[1] The bath can be a great transition to bedtime for your baby because his body temperature cools by a few degrees after a warm bath, making it easier for him to fall asleep.[2] I witnessed this firsthand on many occasions. Often, I could barely get my baby diapered, clothed, and swaddled after the bath without him falling asleep.

In addition, for newborns, the feeling of warm water in a bath can mimic the sensation of being in the womb. Remember that your baby has spent most of his time inside a warm uterus, and this is the feeling that is comforting and familiar to him.

Once your baby's umbilical cord has dried and fallen off, you can make the leap from sponge bath to a real bath for your baby. If you want to bathe your baby as part of his bedtime routine, plan and prepare before you begin the bath. Make sure you set out a soft towel, clean diaper, change of clothing, and your baby's swaddle blanket before starting the bath. I usually kept a pacifier with the change of clothes also in case my baby started to fuss. If you use diaper cream or any other kind of cream for your baby, keep those near you as well. Being prepared will help you make a seamless transition from your baby's bath to bedtime.

In the first few months, a sink or baby bathtub is the easiest and safest place to bathe your baby. When bathing your baby, pay close attention to the water temperature and use warm, not hot water. According to the American Academy of Pediatrics (AAP), the faucet temperature should not exceed 120 degrees Fahrenheit to prevent burns, so you may want to adjust your water heater settings accordingly.[3] Fill the sink or baby bath with water *before* placing your baby in the bath in case the water temperature is too hot or too cold. Always test the water temperature with your hand or inside of your wrist before putting your baby in the bath.

The first time you bathe your baby, it can seem rather awkward, since his tiny body can be slippery and difficult to hold. Try easing your baby feetfirst into the baby bathtub or sink. Put one of your hands under his bottom to support him and use your other hand to cradle his head and neck. Most importantly, never leave your baby unattended in the bath, even for a second. Always keep one of your hands on your baby's body, and do not let yourself get distracted by anything else during your baby's bath time.

Use a gentle, mild soap to cleanse your baby. Many moms prefer to use fragrance-free, hypoallergenic products with their babies, since some infants can have sensitive skin. Although it is not necessary to bathe your baby every day, you can still incorporate a bath into your bedtime routine a few days a week. If you choose to bathe him every day, consider alternating the days when you use soap on your baby's body and apply a small amount of hypoallergenic moisturizing lotion on your baby's skin after the bath. If you are using a washcloth, make sure it is soft and take care to wash your baby's body very gently. Avoid scrubbing or rubbing any part of your baby's body and always use a delicate touch when bathing him.

A bath can be a calming and relaxing step in your baby's bedtime routine, and it is something that you can continue in his bedtime routine as he grows.

15

BEDTIME ROUTINE TIP 8: DROWSY NOT DREAMING

Newborns sleep so much that it is usually not a challenge to get them to sleep. They fall asleep easily in their first few weeks, and you can often place them in their crib to sleep without any difficulty. They may not stay asleep for long durations in the beginning, but they do fall asleep easily in most cases. After the first few weeks, your baby will become more alert, and it may take more effort to get him to sleep. Having a strong sleep routine will help you and your baby develop a positive pattern of behaviors that promote consistent sleep. However, you still need to work with your baby's sleep cues to know when the best moment is to try to put him to sleep, and that is when he is drowsy, not dreaming.

Putting your baby to sleep when he is drowsy, instead of when he is asleep, enables your baby to develop the ability to self-soothe at night and put himself back to sleep without parental intervention.[1] Yes, your baby may still cry and fuss at times, but providing him with the opportunity to fall asleep on his own will enable him to establish predictable sleep patterns. Your baby will learn to fall asleep without being held or rocked to sleep every time and will trust that you will be there again when he wakes up to feed, hold, and comfort him.

When your baby is awake, pay attention for cues that your baby is drowsy, such as yawning, staring, closing his eyes, rubbing his eyes, fussing, or crying. As soon as you notice these cues, start your baby's bedtime routine. When putting your baby to bed, singing, cuddling, and rocking are all ways to relax your baby and ease the transition from wake time to sleep time. However, try to put your baby in his bed when he is drowsy and before he is asleep. If you are having a difficult time spotting your baby's drowsy signals, keeping a log of your baby's sleep, as discussed in Chapter 6, can help you remember when the next nap time is approaching. When your baby is less than two months old, two hours of wakefulness is usually the maximum amount of time that he can stay awake without being overtired.[2] When I observed my own babies and reviewed their sleep logs, I found this research to be spot-on, since my babies routinely showed signs of drowsiness after ninety to one hundred minutes of wakefulness. As you and your baby develop a routine, you will find that your baby will become tired around the same times every day, which will make it easier for you to know when he is drowsy and ready for sleep.

It can be tempting to rock or nurse your baby to sleep, as a method of soothing your baby, before every nap and bedtime. The pitfall is that your baby will learn to rely on being held or nursed to fall asleep and may have a difficult time falling asleep without your intervention. He may also have difficulty going back to sleep on his own after normal nighttime awakenings or stirrings.[3] Even if your baby cries or fusses when you initially put him in his crib, if he is tired, he will learn to fall asleep on his own.

Since you want to encourage your baby to fall asleep on his own, eliminate any unnecessary distractions, such as a mobile above his bed or cuddly animals attached to the sides of the crib. As cute as they may look, the mobile (especially if it moves and plays music) and other decorative items are stimulating and will make it more difficult for your baby to relax and fall asleep.

By using the tips described in this and the previous chapters, you will establish a strong sleep routine and help your baby learn to fall asleep on his own. It may take a few times for him to accomplish this. He may wake and cry and go back to sleep. It may take him anywhere from five to twenty minutes to calm himself and fall asleep. All babies are different, but the more they are able to fall asleep on their own without constant intervention from you, the more consistent and predictable their sleep patterns will be. If you are still having trouble getting your baby to fall asleep and stay asleep, consider the practice of sleep training, which I will discuss next.

16

BEDTIME ROUTINE TIP 9: SLEEP TRAINING

As your baby reaches eight to twelve weeks of age, he may be sleeping through the night. "Sleeping through the night" varies by each person's interpretation, but it is commonly understood to mean that your baby is sleeping at least a six-hour stretch during normal night-time hours, for example, midnight to 6:00 a.m., or 11:00 p.m. to 5:30 a.m. If your baby is not sleeping for a five- to six-hour stretch by eight to twelve weeks, you may consider sleep training.

The views on infant sleep training, in particular the cry-it-out method, vary widely. I understand fully that sleep training does not align with every parent's philosophy. However, I am a firm believer in various methods of sleep training for infants after eight weeks of age. For me, it was an easy decision because I knew it would have a positive and significant lasting effect on our entire family. I wanted more sleep. My husband wanted more sleep. I wanted my baby to learn to fall asleep on his own and sleep longer. Once I had my second child, I did not want my first child to be awakened by a crying baby in the middle of the night. I also observed that my baby was generally happier when he had more sleep. All these reasons supported our decision to sleep train our babies.

When I use the phrase "cry-it-out," I am referring to the method of sleep training where you let your baby cry until he falls asleep without any assistance from you. Some parents choose to use this cry-it-out or "extinction" approach when their baby has difficulty falling asleep for his nap or nighttime sleep. Other parents use this method when they are trying to wean their baby off the night feeding or when their baby wakes repeatedly during the night for attention or stimulation after he has already stopped taking a nighttime feeding. In my experience, sleep training by the cry-it-out method usually takes anywhere from three to five nights. Instead of rocking your baby back to sleep, or giving your baby a bottle or the breast, you allow your baby to cry himself to sleep. Yes, it may seem insensitive and severe to some parents, including myself when I first heard about this method. However, keep in mind that this is a tiny sliver of time in the larger scheme of things. I will warn you that those first few nights of sleep training may feel like the longest nights of your life. I recommend having a set of earplugs and a white noise machine. You may even want to sleep in a different room to avoid the crying. I do not think I slept at all during the first night we did the cry-it-out method with my daughter. Even when she finally fell asleep, I was anticipating her next cry. The second night, my daughter's crying was louder but shorter in duration. By the third night, she cried for about thirty minutes and then slept for seven hours straight without waking.

My second child loved his pacifier, so we used it as our method of sleep training him. When we were ready to wean him off the night feeding at eight weeks old, I gave him his pacifier when he woke for his 3:00 a.m. feeding. I went in quickly, quietly, without interacting with him, reinserted the pacifier, and walked out. My intent was to see if the sensation of sucking on the pacifier would replace that of a bottle or breast. I was confident that he did not need the extra feeding anymore, and I wanted to test it out. The first night, I had to go into his room four times to reinsert the pacifier. The second and third nights, I had to give him his pacifier once when he cried at his usual 3:00 a.m. awakening, and he went back to sleep until 6:00 a.m. The fourth night, he and I both slept through the night until 6:00 a.m.

There are several books that discuss different approaches to sleep training, and I encourage you to read more about the advantages and disadvantages for your baby and your family.[1] For example, Dr. Richard Ferber discusses a more gradual approach to sleep training in his widely-recognized book, <u>Solve Your Child's Sleep Problems</u>. The "Ferber method" involves letting your baby cry for a few minutes and checking on him to briefly comfort him at set intervals of time. The intent is to gradually increase the time between each check-in and teach your baby to fall asleep on his own.

Is it simple to sleep train your baby? Yes. Will it be emotionally difficult for you during the process? Highly likely. Is it worth the crying and frustration for a few nights? Absolutely. I do not regret sleep training any of my children. It was one of the best parenting decisions that we made when our children were babies.

PART 3: FUSSINESS

"Parenting is hard, and the struggles can sometimes feel like they overshadow the joys. Knowing that struggling is normal and will pass helps us get through the hard times so we can truly treasure the good ones."

— L. R. KNOST

Every baby will cry and be inconsolable at some point in his infancy. Some babies are fussier than others, but every single mother will deal with a fussy baby at some point during motherhood. This is normal and expected, but the good news is that there are many ways to minimize your baby's fussiness. As a mom of four children, I found that when you have a baby, you need to be creative and find solutions to help make your life easier, even if those solutions are unconventional. In the following chapters, I will discuss the techniques that worked best for me in the hopes that they will work for you and your baby too.

17

TOOLS TO REDUCE FUSSINESS

Crying can cause new mothers to feel stressed and frustrated. However, a study that considered new mothers' confidence, mood, and stress in the first three months of parenthood found that all these symptoms improved over time for the majority of the subjects.[1] As your baby develops and changes rapidly in the first six months, you will adapt and change also.

Remind yourself that the newborn months are *temporary*. In addition, there are hundreds of reasons why babies get frustrated and cry. The baby might be too cold or too warm. The air might be too dry. The baby needs a diaper change. He needs to be burped or has indigestion. He is constantly spitting up. There may be too much noise when he is trying to sleep. The baby's sleep environment may be too bright or too quiet. The baby's clothing might be scratchy or uncomfortable. His swaddle might have come undone, and he is focused on moving his legs rather than sleeping. His pacifier may have fallen out. The baby may suffer from colic (like my daughter did) and just seems to cry for no reason at all most of the day. I can keep going, but the list will never end.

If your baby is often fussy and appears to be in discomfort after eating, he may be experiencing gastroesophageal reflux disease

(GERD) or simply known as "reflux." When babies suffer from reflux, the acid in their stomach backs up into the esophagus or throat, causing frequent spitting up and irritation of the esophagus.[2] As a result, babies with reflux tend to cry and fuss more after feeding than babies who do not have reflux. If you notice that your baby's fussiness is often during or after feeding times, accompanied by other factors such as spitting up, crying, arching his back while feeding, or pushing the bottle or breast away, your baby may be experiencing GERD.

Do not panic. Even the fussiest, most colicky baby can be calmed. Some babies require more effort to calm than others, and often it is a game of trial and error to find what works for your baby. The good news is that there is a multitude of things you can do to minimize your baby's fussiness, many of which I have already discussed in this book, so you are already armed with tools to calm your baby. On that note, I will discuss how some of these same tools can help you manage your baby's crying and fussiness.

1. Often, a change of scenery alone is a cure for fussiness. Using a stroller can help fussiness because babies benefit from a change in environment, fresh air, and some movement.
2. The pacifier is my ultimate go-to for fussiness. Try, try, and try again until your baby takes the pacifier. This will minimize your baby's crying and your own frustration from hearing the crying.
3. Swaddling will reduce your baby's fussiness and crying at night.
4. Keep your child on a feeding schedule and try to ensure your baby has a full feeding. This will also give your baby more opportunity for content playtime.
5. Carrying your baby in a sling or baby carrier can help with fussiness. The baby feels the closeness of the parent while having some light movement as you walk around, sway side to side, or lightly bounce while sitting down. My baby would be very fussy when I first put him in the sling for about five

minutes, and then he would stop almost immediately and fall into a calm, restful state.

6. Sing to your baby. Songs are even more effective than speech in reducing infant distress.[3] In one study by the University of Montreal, infants remained calm twice as long when listening to a song as they did when listening to speech.[4] Parents tend to speak to their babies more often than sing, and this study suggests that singing more often may help your baby regulate his emotions.[5]

7. Having a bedtime routine will help calm your baby because he will grow accustomed to the routine you have created and look forward to the time with you. Knowing "what comes next" in their day is calming for babies (and most toddlers and older children too!).

8. If your baby has reflux, you can do the following after each feeding to minimize his discomfort: keep him upright, avoid bouncing him, and burp him regularly. You can put a small, folded blanket or pillow under the crib sheet or mattress pad on your baby's crib to give the bed a subtle incline. This can help prevent your baby from spitting up and crying due to discomfort while he is sleeping. There are also medications that your pediatrician can prescribe that will reduce or neutralize stomach acids to help with your baby's GERD.

18

CALMING YOUR FUSSY BABY WITH MOVEMENT AND CONNECTION

In addition to the tools described in Chapter 17, there are several other techniques that can calm a fussy baby. These techniques incorporate motion or physical connection with your baby, sometimes both.

1. If you have (or can borrow) a big exercise ball, sit on it and bounce lightly while holding your baby. You can do this by holding your baby in your arms or by putting him in a carrier or sling while gently bouncing on the exercise ball. The rhythmic motion can help calm a fussy baby. When my first son was between six and eight weeks old, I did this every evening around 6:00 p.m. for twenty minutes because that was his fussiest time.

2. Using a rocking chair or glider chair can help calm a fussy baby while giving your own body a break by sitting down. Most babies enjoy the rocking motion, especially when they are fussy. Propping up a pillow under your elbow can give your arms a rest while you continue to hold or feed your baby. Few people tell you how exhausting it can be to carry and rock your baby. I logged many miles pacing back and forth while gently bouncing my colicky baby, so the glider was a

relief for me. A rocking chair or glider enables you to nurse or give your baby a bottle, sing to him, read to him, or just hold him, all while providing a gentle rocking motion to calm him.

3. Infant massage is becoming a popular way to soothe a fussy baby. I discovered that gently touching my son's forehead and cheeks and using my finger to trace the outline of his face were calming for him. The gentle strokes on his face and head soothed him when he was upset and fussy. There are many techniques for infant massage that are readily available online. In addition to calming your baby, infant massage also helps you bond with your baby by allowing you to focus solely on calming him through your touch. Massaging your baby helps you connect with your baby, calm him, and may give him relief from gas and colic.[1] Massage may also promote better sleep patterns, decrease stress hormones, and help with teething and stomach discomfort that your baby may be experiencing.[2]

4. Baby swings, bouncer chairs, or simply driving around in your car can have a similar effect as a stroller or carrier by providing some movement for your baby to reduce fussiness. The swing, bouncer, and car seat also give new moms a break (and your arms a rest), which is a consideration that should not be overlooked. Since baby swings are appropriate for only a short period of time, consider borrowing one for your baby. Many new parents have used them and are willing to share or pass their swing along. A friend of mine gave us their baby swing, and I passed it along to another family when we were finished with it. The baby swing can provide tremendous relief from crying for new parents in the first two months. The baby will often fall asleep in the swing. Sometimes, even if the baby does not sleep, he will become calm and relaxed by the movement of the swing. Some swings have several speeds, music, different directions of swinging, and other accessories; however, a basic baby swing that gently moves your baby back and forth to create a lulling pattern of movement is sufficient. Try to avoid putting your baby in the swing for every nap,

since it will make it increasingly difficult for the baby to become comfortable in his crib to sleep. Your goal should be for your baby to fall asleep without assistance from motion by the time he is three months old. However, when your baby is a newborn, using a swing is unlikely to have a negative impact on his developing sleep habits. The swing is an excellent way to reduce fussiness and promote sleep when you have tried other methods first. Try to use it as a last resort and not as the easy crutch for every nap.

5. Taking a bath or shower with your baby can also help reduce fussiness. I even nursed my first son in the bathtub a few times when he was fussy and suffering from reflux, and it worked like a charm every time. This approach may sound odd, but it worked.

6. Play music in your home and in the car when your baby is fussy. Hold your baby and dance with him to the music. Sometimes, I would play loud rock music and my baby calmed down. Other times, I would play classical piano music, and this would sooth him. Sometimes, instrumental lullabies were the magic ingredient to stop the crying. There are also many music albums made specifically to calm fussy babies. Music is one of the best tools you can use with babies. It can be used to entertain them, soothe them, and improve their overall disposition. As your baby starts to calm down and exhibit less fussiness, you may notice a change in your own mood as well.

When your baby cries for long periods of time, it can feel stressful. Remember that you are not alone, and it is perfectly normal to get frustrated when your baby cries. Some babies cry more than others, but *every* mom has dealt with a fussy, crying baby. It is important to allow yourself to take a break from your baby when he is fussy. If you find yourself feeling overwhelmed or angry, call a neighbor or a friend to come over to help you. It is acceptable and encouraged to ask another adult to hold your baby, give him a bottle, or push him in the stroller to give you a break from the crying.

If you do not have anyone to help you at a time when you feel upset and anxious, put your baby in his crib, bouncer chair, or other safe place, and take a short break in another room. You can let your baby cry for a few minutes while you take a few deep breaths and reset. You may need to do this a few times a day if it helps reduce your frustration with your baby's fussiness. Taking care of yourself will help you be a better mom to your baby, which I will discuss further in Part 4.

PART 4: TAKING CARE OF YOURSELF

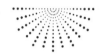

"Being a mother, as far as I can tell, is a constantly evolving process of adapting to the needs of your child while also changing and growing as a person in your own right."

— DEBORAH INSEL

Self-care means something different to everyone. For some people, it may mean simply taking care of themselves by practicing proper hygiene and eating a healthy diet. For others, self-care involves getting outside every day to exercise. For those focused more on mental health, self-care may include meditation, religion, reading, or therapy. As a mother, I define self-care as caring for your whole self, which includes your physical, mental, and spiritual health. When I make self-care a priority, I function better as a mom because I am healthier, happier, and more confident.

19

NAPS

When you become a mother, people will tell you to sleep when the baby sleeps. This makes sense in theory, but I found that I could not always sleep when my baby was sleeping. Sometimes, I simply was not tired, or I was overtired and could not wind down enough to sleep. Other times, I had things I wanted to do that were more important to me than taking a nap. However, when I had a newborn to care for, I always needed a nap at some point every day, even if it was for just twenty minutes. Taking a nap, even if it is just resting on the couch with your eyes closed, is rejuvenating when you have a newborn. Daytime naps are healthy for new mothers because they give you a much-needed break to do absolutely nothing. Taking a short power nap of thirty minutes or less can help you feel not as tired and stressed and can have a positive effect on your mood. One study that analyzed daytime naps found that short naps can even restore wakefulness and enhance performance and learning ability.[1]

If you were not used to taking naps before you had children, it can seem awkward to get into a routine of napping. However, as the weeks go on, you will find yourself looking forward to a nap every day. You may feel so tired that you could sleep anywhere. After I had my second child, I remember falling asleep on our playroom floor while trying to read a book to my toddler because I literally could not keep my eyes open. Your body and your mind both need a break when you have a newborn. A daytime nap is a necessary and well-deserved pause when you are spending every other waking moment with your baby.

Babies tend to nap every couple of hours in the first few months. Just weeks after my baby was born, I discovered that I no longer needed to rest during his first morning naps, because I had more energy earlier in the day and wanted to get things done. However, once afternoon hit, I was desperate for a nap. Most days, I would take a short nap when my baby took his first afternoon nap. If you are keeping a log of your baby's sleep times, it will make it easier for you to carve out time to nap. Try to fit in at least one time each day when you can nap or rest without your phone or any other distractions.

Find a quiet, dark place to nap. Using an eye mask or putting a cloth over your eyes is another option if you do not have a dark place to nap during the day. Turn off the television and music. Your bedroom, or any room in which you nap, will function more effectively as a place for quality sleep if you minimize or remove electronic devices. The blue light emitted from certain electronic devices, such as televisions, computers, and cell phones, can make it more difficult to fall asleep. Put your phone, tablet, headphones, and any other devices away. Silence them, put them in sleep mode, and move them out of arm's reach. Ideally, leave them in another room unless you need to set an alarm for yourself to wake up at a certain time. It can be tempting to lie down with your phone with the intent of just checking a few emails or texts. However, there are no guarantees on the duration of your baby's nap, so unplug from technology. Otherwise, before you know it, thirty minutes have come and gone, the baby is awake, and you have not given yourself the rest you need and deserve. Now, not only will you be tired, but you will be frustrated because you missed your opportunity to nap.

Even twenty or thirty minutes of daily rest time can have a significant and positive impact on you. You may need to nap a few times a day when your baby is a newborn. Make napping a priority for you. If it helps you, consider writing "take a nap" on your daily to-do list. Create a schedule that allows you to nap every day when you have a baby. It will help you feel recharged, both physically and mentally.

20

NIGHTTIME SLEEP

I love Amy Poehler's reference to sleep during motherhood when she said, "Sleep at this point is just a concept, something I'm looking forward to investigating in the future." All joking aside, unless you have a full-time night nurse feeding your baby every night, the unavoidable truth is that your sleep will be shorter and fragmented with a newborn. However, there are ways to maximize the amount and quality of your sleep. Many of the same techniques used to encourage your baby to sleep can even be applied to your own sleep routine.

1. As discussed in Chapter 19, remove electronic devices from your bedroom or put them in sleep mode. Once you have a baby, it is highly unlikely that you will need an alarm on your phone to wake you for many years.
2. Keep the room dark and cool. Use blinds, shades, or curtains, since your nighttime hours of sleep may start earlier or end later than what you were used to before you had a baby.
3. Third, use a white noise machine to block out unwanted sounds.
4. Limit your caffeine intake in the afternoon and evening and replace it with water. The effects of caffeine can take several

hours to wear off. As a result, caffeine can disrupt your ability to fall asleep, which is the last thing you want at night with a baby.

5. Eating large meals late at night can cause indigestion and heartburn, which will make it more difficult to fall and stay asleep. As a guideline, the US National Library of Medicine recommends avoiding large meals two hours before you go to bed.

6. Try to limit your alcohol intake before going to bed. Alcohol is a sedative which can cause you to fall asleep quickly. However, your REM sleep phase can be adversely affected by alcohol, which can result in more sleep disruptions and shorter sleep duration.[1]

7. After your baby's last evening feeding, go to bed. Do not stay up checking emails or watching a movie. When your baby goes to sleep in the evening, even if it is a stretch of two to four hours, you should go to sleep also. As your baby grows, her stretches of sleep at night will increase in duration, and that nighttime period will be your opportunity for a longer stretch of sleep too.

Even keeping a to-do list each day can help improve your sleep. By writing down tasks before you go to bed, you can relieve some of your stress and allow your mind to relax and prepare for sleep. If you keep a pad of paper and pen next to your bed, you can jot down tasks or notes for the next day. By doing this, you will not have to worry about remembering what you must do in the morning, and it will free some space in your mind for more peaceful thoughts.

If you find yourself having difficulty falling back asleep after your baby wakes during the night or feeling too anxious to sleep, it may be helpful to contact a health care professional for advice. Many women have difficulty falling asleep and staying asleep, even when they are exhausted, and a health care professional can help get you back on track. Many new mothers struggle with insomnia, which is defined as persistent difficulty with sleep onset or maintenance, consolidation, or quality of sleep. Hormonal changes and postpartum depression, which can involve anxiety, sadness, and difficulty falling asleep and awakening, can also prevent you from achieving quality sleep.[2] In any of these situations, it is important for you to seek the help you need. Taking the time care for yourself and achieve better sleep will enable you to be a better mother to your baby.

21

EXERCISE

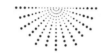

One of the best things you can do to take care of yourself as a new mom is find a way to incorporate daily exercise into your life. Whether you prefer to exercise indoors or outdoors, your physical and mental health will reap the benefits. If you can get outside to exercise, the benefits are even greater. Find a way, even for just a short time every day, to work up a sweat. For some moms with newborns, this can seem challenging and discouraging because you may feel tired and overwhelmed. However, exercise does not have to be overwhelming. Learning to move your body in fun and enjoyable ways is easier than you may think.

Some people have the misconception that they do not have enough energy to exercise or that they will be more tired after exercising. The interesting fact about exercise is that it actually gives you more energy for the other things you want to do. Physical inactivity can lead to fatigue, increased body weight, decreased energy, and a higher risk of developing health conditions.[1] When you exercise, your body releases chemicals called endorphins, which reduce your perception of pain and improve your mood.[2] Exercise is an excellent way to relieve stress, anxiety, and frustration and helps you sleep longer and more soundly. Exercise helps keep your bones, joints, and muscles strong and healthy so you are able to perform your daily activities, including taking care of your baby and your family.[3] Postpartum exercise can also reduce your fatigue, improve your mood and mental acuity, and help you reach a healthy weight. [4] In addition to helping you stay fit, exercise decreases your risk for developing heart disease, stroke, diabetes, dementia, depression, and many cancers, among other chronic health conditions.[5] Further, exercise can help you establish a healthy routine in your life. You may be surprised to find that your body responds positively to exercise and that you feel lethargic on the days you skip exercising.

The American College of Obstetricians and Gynecologists (ACOG) recommends that postpartum women get a minimum of two and a half hours of moderate-intensity aerobic activity every week.[6] Moderate-intensity aerobic activity is movement that results in sweating and increased heart rate. That might seem like a tall order, but if you divide that number up over a week's time, it is quite easy to achieve. For women who experience a normal, vaginal delivery, it is generally fine to resume light exercise within a few days of giving birth. However, few mothers want to start that soon, so give yourself time to recover from the experience of childbirth and resume exercise gradually when your body feels ready. If you had a cesarean delivery or experienced other complications, you should discuss starting an exercise program with your doctor to find a timeline that works for you.

If you can incorporate some kind of exercise outdoors, even a few times per week, your mind and body will thank you for it. It is easy to fall into the endless cycle of feeding, changing, and sleeping without leaving your home. However, this will leave you exhausted and run down. Leaving your home to exercise will help you feel refreshed and recharged. Light affects you in a positive way by literally brightening your mood. Sunlight helps maintain your serotonin levels, which in turn can increase your energy and help you be more positive, focused, and calm. One study showed that even a short time of outdoor activity gives your self-esteem and mood a boost.[7] Whenever you can walk or be outside close to nature, especially near water, the effect on your mood is even greater.[8] Some of this may be attributable to the vitamin D production in our bodies through exposure to sunlight, which you cannot get from working out inside your home or at the gym. Research has established a link between low vitamin D levels and depression and other mental illness, so it is important to maintain a healthy dose of vitamin D.[9]

According to a 2013 Duke Medicine study, children whose mothers encourage them to exercise and eat well, and model those healthy behaviors for their children, are more likely to be active and healthy eaters.[10] By including exercise in your daily routine, you are making physical and mental health a priority for you and your family.

I am not suggesting you adopt an intensive exercise program when you have a newborn. Rather, I am encouraging you to find a positive way to take care of yourself by doing some kind of physical activity. The easiest way to incorporate some exercise into your life when you have a newborn is to include your baby. Finding a way to exercise with a newborn is easier than you might think, and there are many options for maintaining or improving your level of fitness. Of course, if you are fortunate to have childcare, or family or friends to help you with your baby, take advantage of that time to go for a walk or do some kind of exercise on your own. However, when you do not have help, there are ways to incorporate exercise into your life with your newborn that involve minimal effort and time. Perhaps start with a twenty minute walk every day. This can be done with your baby in a stroller or carrier and will enable you to get outside and exercise with your baby. That is an accomplishment for any new mom!

The point is to start with an exercise routine that is manageable and not overwhelming for you. This is important for new mothers, since we often feel guilty about doing anything for ourselves. You may consider finding a friend or neighbor to walk or jog with you and your baby, perhaps even another mom with an infant. Making plans to exercise with someone else keeps you accountable. Many moms groups have smaller subgroups of moms who walk or run together. Stroller Strides and other fitness groups for moms seem to be popping up everywhere, making it easier and more convenient for moms to get fit and exercise together. Having the support of other moms in a group setting is both motivating and comforting.

Doing online workout programs at home is popular with many new moms who feel overwhelmed and self-conscious about starting an exercise program. These work well because you can set your own schedule and define the type of workout that suits you. Many exercise programs even offer a free trial for a few months so you can try them out before committing to anything. Until your baby is mobile, there are often opportunities to fit in some yoga, stretching, or a short exercise video, even when your baby is awake. Whether she is in a bouncer chair or lying on a play mat, you can be within a few steps of her while still doing something positive for your body. To create your own simple workouts, use the stairs in or near your home. You can run, or walk quickly, up and down the stairs for twenty minutes, or even with your baby in a baby carrier, which provides a great leg and cardio workout. Exercises such as planks, wall sits, lunges, and push-ups are great ways to strengthen your body anytime at home. Consider borrowing or purchasing exercise equipment, such as a yoga mat (which is great for almost any kind of stretching, yoga, core work, or exercise videos), an exercise ball (which also has other uses as described in Part 3), a jump rope, or free weights to make your home workouts convenient and effective for you. Another benefit of most of these at-home exercises is that they are free or require minimal financial investment.

Many gyms and fitness centers offer their members on-site childcare, which enables moms to have personal time to exercise. When your baby is under three months of age, much of her time is spent sleeping anyway. Bring your baby supply stash and allow yourself to take an hour or two to exercise and shower, knowing that your baby is in a safe place in close proximity to you. Taking an exercise class at the gym also enables you to have social interaction with other adults, which can be a well-deserved break in your day. In addition, exposing your baby to new voices and faces when she is an infant is an excellent way to help her become comfortable around people outside of your family and primary caregivers.

Exercise plays an instrumental role in my physical and mental health, and it helps me be a better mom each day. Every single time I made a point to get outside to exercise, my outlook and attitude were more positive than before I started. Whatever doubts and frustrations I had before I left the house seemed less overwhelming and more manageable after I spent some time outside.

Exercise is a key element to maintaining your mental and physical health during motherhood. If you include physical activity in your daily routine, preferably outside, you will be able to continue this routine as your baby grows. Establishing a healthy lifestyle not only helps your own physical and mental health, but it also sets a positive example for your entire family.

22

HYDRATION

We hear about the importance of water all the time. We know water is necessary for our survival. In fact, water is the primary chemical component in our bodies, comprising between fifty to seventy percent of our body weight. Consumption of an adequate amount of water each day is essential to our health.

I was a competitive runner for almost twenty years, so I am a firm believer in the benefits of water. Insufficient water intake can lead to moodiness, headaches, dizziness, constipation, and dehydration. As a new mom, you may already be experiencing mood swings due to the hormonal changes in your body, and the last thing you want is to bring additional moodiness from dehydration into the mix.

Drinking more water can also help you maintain a healthy weight if you use it to replace sugary and high-calorie drinks. One study found that individuals who increased their consumption of plain water by just one percent had a decrease in their total daily calorie intake and their consumption of beverages and foods with saturated fat, sugar, sodium, and cholesterol.[1]

Drinking water throughout the day helps your body maintain the correct balance of fluids. Water also helps you recover from physical activity and prevents muscle fatigue. The list of benefits from drinking water does not stop there. Water aids in the digestive process, cushions joints, protects organs and tissues, flushes bacteria from your bladder, maintains electrolyte balance, stabilizes your heartbeat and blood pressure, and helps regulate body temperature.[2] Drinking water is a simple step in your daily routine to keep your entire body functioning better overall.

As a new mother, you may feel exhausted and run down. If your body is dehydrated, it will only add to your feelings of exhaustion. Staying hydrated is an easy way to keep your body functioning well and healthy when you have a baby.

Getting enough water is important for all new moms, but how much water should you be drinking each day? Generally, women should consume about 11.5 cups (2.7 liters) of water each day according to the US National Academies of Sciences, Engineering, and Medicine. However, about twenty percent of our fluid intake comes from the food we consume, so drinking about eight glasses of water per day is a good rule of thumb to follow.[3] That may seem like a lot of water, but if you spread it out over a day, it is easy to achieve. All new moms can benefit from staying properly hydrated, but drinking water is especially important for nursing mothers. If you do not have enough healthy fluids in your body, your milk supply may be affected adversely. In addition, if you live in a warm climate, or exercise frequently, you should increase your daily water intake accordingly.

I remember feeling thirsty constantly when I was breastfeeding my babies. I found that a simple way to stay hydrated is to fill a large water bottle each morning. Keep your water bottle with you wherever you go and drink from it throughout the day. Bring your water bottle in the car, put it in the stroller and near your bedside, and keep it near you when you exercise. Your water bottle should be on your checklist of things you need to take with you when you leave the house. Another way to remember to stay hydrated throughout the day is to drink water every time you nurse or give your baby a bottle. Since babies feed frequently, I found this to be an easy way to stay hydrated.

If drinking plain water is not appealing to you, you can add mint leaves, cucumber, or fruit slices, such as lemon, lime, or orange to give it a fresh twist. Make a point to drink water throughout the day rather than waiting until you feel thirsty. Once you are thirsty, or you notice that your urine is bright yellow, your body is telling you that you have not consumed enough water. Staying hydrated is an important part of self-care for all new moms, and it is easy to achieve if you make it part of your daily routine.

23

SOCIAL INTERACTION

When you have a new baby, your world changes. Your responsibilities multiply. Your social circle may diminish in size for a while. It can be easy to fall into a routine of interacting only with your baby and your partner. Why do new parents do this? Many mothers feel both overwhelmed with responsibility and overtired. They may lack confidence in their ability as a parent. These are all normal feelings. After all, it can be hard to motivate yourself to engage in social circles with a new baby when you are tired. You can boost your confidence levels and feel less overwhelmed by interacting with other moms, who have babies similar in age to your own, and finding a sense of community with them.

By interacting with other moms, you will find that you share similar frustrations, joys, and doubts. Having other moms with whom you can communicate these feelings, and who understand because they are in a similar situation, will benefit all of you. Engaging in adult conversation, even if the topic is something related to your baby (which it most likely will be!), is refreshing and important for your mental health. In fact, moms without social support have an increased risk for postpartum depression.[1] Even when you feel overwhelmed or exhausted, consider reaching out to other moms to support you and help you through each stage with your baby.

If you are fortunate to have nearby friends and neighbors with babies or young children, make it a priority to get together with them on a regular basis, even if it is just for an hour. Put it on your to-do list. Even if your conversation takes place while both of you nurse and change diapers, social interaction with other adults is important. Schedule times to meet at each other's homes or walk together with your babies in strollers or carriers.

If you do not have friends nearby with babies, here are a few simple ways to meet other moms with whom you can interact.

MOMS GROUPS

In my experience, one of the best ways to meet other new moms is through a local mothers group. Some of my closest friends today are women I met in my moms group over ten years ago. Engaging with other women who had newborns was a key part of my growth and awareness as a new mom. Spending time with other moms at each other's homes provided a comfortable forum for all of us to express our frustrations, concerns, and excitement. After all, what other group of people could genuinely share your excitement over getting a five-hour uninterrupted stretch of sleep? Who else could possibly understand how you feel when your newborn spits up all over you multiple times every day because she has reflux?

These women were, and still are, my rocks. I developed a level of comfort with these women that was different from my other friendships. We were all tired, wearing milk-stained clothing, and had no idea what we were doing as new mothers. Every experience we shared with each other was helpful because we were all thirsty for information that might make our lives easier as new moms. We shared a closeness that was unparalleled because we were doing the most important work of our lives together.

If you join a moms group, your baby will also begin interacting with other babies and adults. This may seem unimportant in your baby's first few months, but when you provide your baby opportunities for social interactions with other people, you are laying the groundwork for her development.

Many cities have chapters of parent groups based on the area in which you live. Some other groups are organized through community sites such as Nextdoor or Facebook. One of the best resources for finding groups is other moms who have older children and who can recommend groups in your area. In my area, several friends who had children before I did recommended a local group called Las Madres[2]. Las Madres organizes groups for moms based on where you live and your baby's birth year. This system works well because you join a group of other women going through similar experiences, and your babies are of similar ages. Living in the same general area makes it easier to plan playdates and social events with these moms. The moms with multiple children, or who have babies a few months older than your own baby, are often the best sources of information because they have already conquered the current stage that you are in with your own baby. For example, if your baby is starting to roll over in her crib (and thus waking herself up repeatedly), there is usually another mom who has already been through that developmental stage and is willing to offer advice and encouragement. Confiding in, and seeking advice from other moms, can leave you feeling refreshed, positive, and understood.

Both you and your baby can benefit from the experience of being in a moms group. You may form lifelong friendships with the women you meet in your group, as I did. In addition, since your children will be the same age, they may attend school and participate in activities together as they grow older. Even today, my children have playdates with others they met in my moms group and they still share a close bond with those children ten years later.

LIBRARY PROGRAMS

Most public libraries offer free children's programs, such as story time, play groups, music programs, and crafts. Usually, there is a weekly story time or music program designated just for babies and their parents. These activities are an excellent way to meet other new parents in a relaxed and nurturing environment. There may be other babies crying, nursing, taking a bottle, or sleeping, and there are virtually no expectations of you, as the parent, other than to sit with your baby and listen to someone read stories, and sometimes sing songs, to the group.

Library story time can provide a break for you by allowing you to sit down and enjoy someone else entertaining your baby. In addition, library programs can be a fun way to introduce your baby to books in a casual setting while interacting with other parents. You may pick up a few tips from other parents while you are there and find comfort in sharing frustrations and new milestones with them.

MUSIC CLASSES

Music classes are an enjoyable way to take a break from the daily baby care routine and meet other parents with babies. One study found that babies who participated in interactive music classes with their parents smiled more, showed stronger early communication skills, and exhibited earlier and more sophisticated brain responses to music.[3] By taking your child to a music class, you are interacting with other adults and may find yourself smiling more as well. Music can reduce your own stress level and help calm and entertain your baby. You may develop friendships with other parents in the class. You may also discover that it is comforting to see other parents with their babies and realize that they have similar struggles and frustrations as you do.

Music classes introduce you and your baby to different types of music, various instruments, and songs in languages other than English, and they are an excellent way to expose both of you to a fun environment and build new relationships. You do not have any responsibilities during the class time other than to hold your baby and interact with her while someone else provides the entertainment. Further, your baby will have a stimulating environment to support her social development and communication.

Several of my friends are moms I met in music classes when my children were babies. We continued to take classes together through the years and build relationships outside of music class. I encourage you to try a music class with your baby for both the musical instruction and the social interaction.

CHURCHES

Even if you are not religious or affiliated with a church, many churches have programs open to anyone in the community. Some churches host groups for moms, such as Mothers of Preschoolers (MOPS), or sponsor events or weekly playgroups for moms and their babies. Often, church-sponsored programs are free or suggest a nominal donation to the church. Attending these events and groups can be a great way to meet other moms in your area.

PARENT/CHILD SWIM CLASSES

If you are looking for another idea to get you out of the house and interacting with other parents, many local pools and gyms have parent/baby swim classes. Swim classes are a fun, refreshing way to meet other parents with babies, expose your baby to a new setting, and bond with her. Many programs are open to babies as young as eight weeks.

In addition, swim classes provide the opportunity to introduce your baby to water at an early age. Being in the water with your baby is a wonderful way to connect with your child through skin-to-skin contact and one-on-one attention. Most programs focus on providing a comfortable environment for your baby and introducing parents to the fundamentals of water safety. The instructors help you teach basic swim skills to your baby, such as back floating, submersion, kicking, and other types of movement in the water.

Introductory swim classes are often interactive, incorporating music, toys, and games during the swim session. Socializing with other babies and adults also helps your baby learn how to function in a group setting. Your baby will use a lot of energy moving her body in new ways in the pool. Keep in mind that the exercise and warm water may lead to an increase in your baby's appetite. You may even find that you and your baby sleep longer and more soundly on the days of swim lessons.

Swimming will also help your baby build and strengthen her muscles. In the water, your baby will learn to hold her head up, move her arms, kick her legs, and develop coordination between all these skills. One research study from the Norwegian University of Science and Technology concluded that babies who participated in swim lessons beginning at two to three months of age had better balance and were better at grasping things by age five than babies who did not participate in swim lessons.[4] In addition, swimming will help your baby strengthen her heart and lungs as she learns basic swimming skills.

PARKS

Parents often joke about how their children met in the sandbox as babies. However, parks and playgrounds are actually some of the best places to meet other new parents and find other children with whom your own can interact. The park is a great place to walk with your stroller or carrier or relax with your baby among other parents and their children. I met one of my dearest friends at the park when our babies were only a few weeks old. We realized our babies had birthdays only a few days apart, and we developed a friendship that has spanned over ten years.

Most parks with children's play equipment have bucket-style swings. Once your baby can support herself sitting with good head control, which usually occurs around six to eight months of age, you will be able to take advantage of these infant swings.[5] The swings are a perfect way to introduce your baby to the outside environment and experience a different kind of movement. Since it requires only minimal gentle pushing, it gives you a break and a chance to do something enjoyable with your baby. I remember having many conversations with other moms while pushing our babies in the bucket swings at the playground.

Bring a blanket, large towel, or fold-up play mat, some snacks, and your baby supply stash and invite some other moms and their babies to join you. Outside time with your baby and other new moms can leave you feeling refreshed. It allows you to sit down, enjoy the outdoors, engage in conversation, and expose your baby to a new environment. In addition, your baby may enjoy lying on a blanket and staring up at the sky while being outside in the fresh air. As your baby grows, this is a great way to encourage your baby to kick his legs, roll over, touch his toes, observe new things, and hear interesting sounds. You can feed your baby outside and change him if needed, or your baby can even take a nap.

2 4

HELP

As a new mother, you face a world of uncharted territory. Glennon Doyle said it perfectly: "Parenting is the most important thing to many of us, and so it's also the place we're most vulnerable. We're all a little afraid we're doing it wrong." You may doubt many of your decisions that involve your baby and feel unsure about each new developmental stage that your baby enters. You have a newborn for whom you are responsible, and you may feel that you should be the only person doing everything for your baby.

As the parent, you will indeed be responsible for the care of your baby, but that does not mean you cannot ask for help. When you have a newborn, the thing you need most (besides sleep) is an extra set of hands to help you. Many new mothers feel uncomfortable asking for support and accepting offers from friends or family to help. Once you have a baby, please throw your intentions of being superwoman and doing everything on your own right in the diaper pail.

Many of your neighbors, family, friends, and acquaintances are willing to help. Perhaps they can stop by to hold your baby for an hour or take her for a walk. Accepting their offer will enable you to have a break and do something for yourself, such as shower, go for a walk, or actually sit down to eat a meal. It also gives you an opportunity for adult conversation. Sometimes, just having another adult around can help you feel more positive and less overwhelmed. You are being a responsible parent when you realize you have reached your limit and need help. I remember being pregnant with my second child and my son was about eighteen months old. It had already been a long, frustrating day. On top of that, I felt nauseous and tired. To cap it off, my son ran into the kitchen and threw up multiple times all over the floor, the counters, and me. I felt as if I would break right then and there. I called my mother and begged her to help me. Being the saint that she is, she came over, and together we cleaned up that horrible mess. We all reach our limit from time to time and need to ask for help.

Part of being a good parent is asking for help when you need it (or sometimes, even when you may not think you need it). If someone asks you what they can do to help, avoid saying "I'm fine" or "I can handle it." Instead, say yes. Do not stop, do not hesitate; accept their offer to help, and tell that person specifically what you need. If you have a to-do list, you can simply refer to your list to give your helper a job to do. It could be as simple as picking up a prescription, getting groceries, or folding the laundry. When you have friends or family who are willing to help, they will be happy to have a specific task to do. In the newborn months, you are already exhausted and may not even remember what day it is. If someone offers to bring you a meal, say yes, and express your gratitude for the help. For most mothers of newborns, the last thing you want to do (or have time to do) is cook a meal that takes more than three minutes to prepare.

If you have a spouse or partner, be open with them right from the beginning about the tasks and responsibilities of your household. If you can divide and conquer the tasks that need to be accomplished, it will be easier for both of you. Motherhood is an all-encompassing role, and asking your partner or spouse to help you with daily tasks will enable you to manage your household more effectively. For example, if grocery shopping becomes your spouse's responsibility, it will create more time for you to focus on other household tasks. Find ways to balance the workload and divide tasks based on each person's ability and schedule. You can also divide up certain tasks with your spouse or partner, such as doing the late-night feedings or getting up with the baby during the night. Having a designated night or nights when you know that you can sleep more can reduce your stress and anxiety and help you feel less overwhelmed with responsibility.

If you have family nearby, it is helpful to develop a schedule for family members to help you. Rather than just stopping by unannounced, consider asking a parent or other family member to come on a specific day or morning each week. Knowing that you will have help at a specific time will allow you to plan your days and week and carve out time for things you want to do when your family member arrives to help with the baby.

If you have the financial means, consider hiring someone to help you. Whether this is a babysitter, a nanny, night nurse, or someone to do your grocery shopping, it is well worth every penny spent. Paying someone to help you with your baby is an investment in your physical and mental health. Try to let go of your idea of being the perfect mom and needing to do everything yourself. Mom guilt can be a powerful force, but so is sleep deprivation! Let go of the guilt you may feel and allow others to help you. Replace your feelings of guilt with a promise to do something in return for the people who help you once you are getting more sleep.

There are numerous online resources to help new moms also. Whether it is a breastfeeding class, an instructional video on swaddling, a parent forum, or a postpartum support group, there are many ways to get help from the comfort of your own home. Meal services and grocery delivery are also great ways to reduce your workload and feed your family. Whenever possible, order your baby supplies online and reduce your trips to the store with your baby.

Finding other moms with babies similar in age to your own baby, through moms groups and classes, will help you create a network of friends with whom you can swap childcare. Perhaps your friend will agree to stay with your baby for an hour, and you can do the same for her in return. By doing this, both of you will have a break, and neither of you is spending money on childcare. You are simply trading favors with a friend who probably needs the help as much as you do. As your child gets older, you will be able to schedule playdates with these moms and continue to share childcare. With toddlers, I often found it easier to have other children around because my children were occupied by new people with whom they could interact.

It may be out of your comfort zone to accept or ask for help when you have a baby. Give it a try anyway. In hindsight, I should have accepted more offers to help. Your baby will not love you any less if you ask friends, family, neighbors, or babysitters to help you. In fact, my children always seem to appreciate me more after I have been gone for a while!

25

JOURNALING

CREATING YOUR JOURNAL

As a new mom, you are responsible for the care of another human being twenty-four hours a day, seven days a week. This responsibility can be overwhelming at times, so having an outlet for your thoughts and ideas is essential to maintaining who you are as a person. I am a firm believer in the benefits of journaling. I started keeping a journal as a young girl and have continued to keep journals throughout my life. There were phases of my life when I did not journal as much, and I regret that I did not write more during those times. I cherish being able to look back at what I wrote over the years and reflect upon the good and the bad experiences in my life.

In this book, you have seen that much of my advice depends on making lists and being organized. Keeping a journal is another way to help you be organized by allowing you to prioritize your needs and concerns. Whether it is making a list of your goals or writing down your frustrations, a journal is an excellent way to organize your thoughts, express your feelings and ideas, and document your experiences. Journaling can have a positive effect on your mental health by helping you manage anxiety and depression and reduce stress in your life.[1]

"Expressive writing," which is writing about stressful, traumatic, or emotional topics, has been linked to improvement in mental and physiological health, including blood pressure, liver and lung function, and immune system function.[2] A 1988 study by psychologist James W. Pennebaker, PhD, who has done considerable research in this area, evaluated the connection between expressive writing and physical and mental health. [3] The individuals in his study who wrote about traumatic experiences reported more positive moods and fewer illnesses than those writing about everyday or trivial experiences. These same individuals also had improved cellular immune system function and fewer doctor visits. His research suggests that people writing about painful and upsetting situations experience both physical and mental benefits.[4] In another study, 107 asthma and rheumatoid arthritis patients wrote for twenty minutes for three consecutive days: seventy-one participants wrote about the most stressful event of their lives; the other thirty-six participants in the control group wrote about emotionally neutral topics. Forty-seven percent of the patients who wrote about stressful events showed improvement in their lung function (asthma patients) and reduction in overall disease severity (rheumatoid arthritis patients) compared with those in the control group who showed little to no improvement.[5] According to psychotherapist F. Diane Barth, these studies indicate that daily expressive writing can reduce stress in your life by helping you release your thoughts and process your emotions which can in turn improve your immune system.[6]

Writing down your thoughts and feelings increases your self-awareness. Self-awareness has been defined differently by various researchers, but the general concept is that you are in touch with your own emotional state. Psychologist Tasha Eurich explains that internal self-awareness is how clearly we see our own values, passions, aspirations, fit with our environment, reactions (including thoughts, feelings, behaviors, strengths, and weaknesses), and impact on others, whereas external self-awareness is our understanding of how other people view us.[7] By writing down your doubts, frustrations, goals, and struggles, you become more aware of what you are feeling and experiencing. There is something powerful about reading your own written words. Journaling can shed light on important issues that you need to address and give you a deeper understanding of your feelings and emotions. Reading your journal entries may help you realize that what you are feeling is not as bad as it seemed initially and can help you feel less anxious overall.

I strongly encourage you to get a journal or notebook and start recording whatever is on your mind each day. Some people prefer to keep a journal on their computer or phone using various apps. Whatever form you choose, use your journal as a place where you can be unfiltered and true to your feelings. Since this is something you are doing for yourself, *you* can decide how and when to use it. If the idea of journaling is new to you or seems awkward, put your reservations aside and give it a try. Journaling is a simple way to help you deal with the ups and downs of motherhood and life. There are no rules, and it is never too late to start.

Writing in a journal can be your escape from daily stressful situations. We all have goals, thoughts, frustrations, and feelings that we may not want to share with anyone else. Journaling can help you process your emotions and vent without having to share these feelings with another person. You may be thinking that you do not have time to write in a journal. You do. You may feel that you are much too busy with a million other tasks to do, but you can make the time to journal, and you will be grateful that you did. Every new mom is busy, but you can give yourself permission to take a few minutes to express your thoughts, feelings, fears, or frustrations in your journal. It can help you recalibrate and give you a mental break from the daily baby routine. Take care of yourself, and you will be a better mom.

CREATING A BABY JOURNAL

One of my favorite recommendations to new mothers is to keep a baby journal. After my first son was born, one of my best friends, who is also a mom, strongly encouraged me to keep a journal for my son to document my baby's milestones. I trusted my friend's advice, since she became a mother first, and clearly she had more experience with this parenting thing than I did. I was hesitant at first and thought it would take considerable time to write about my baby on a daily or weekly basis. Honestly, I doubted whether I could squeeze in one more thing to my daily schedule. However, I was wrong. Once I started writing in my son's journal, I loved doing it and kept writing. I realized how important it was to have a record of the seemingly small things.

Every time I sit down to write in one of my children's journals, I look back at some of the previous entries in their journal. I love reading about the funny things they did when they were babies and toddlers. My children often ask me to read an excerpt from their journal to them. It makes them feel special to hear what I wrote about them in their journal.

If you end up having more than one child, your baby journal will also be an invaluable resource for parenting tips. There are many times when I was unsure about one of my younger children's developmental phases, and I used my journals to guide me based on my own recorded experiences. When my second child was close to dropping his morning nap, I read through my journal entries from my first son to remember what I did during that nap transition time. Of course, each child is different, but using my personal experiences to guide me helped me feel more confident about going through each develop-mental phase with my second, third, and fourth children. Your child's journal can also be a helpful tool when other moms ask for advice or tips. It can serve as a personal reference book documenting the important stages and events in your baby's life. Your experiences with your own baby (or babies) may help someone else through a challenging time with their own children. My baby journals are priceless to me and formed the basis for the very book you are reading.

Keeping a baby journal is an easy way to document important stages and accomplishments in your baby's life. I still prefer pen and paper, but there are multiple online journal options and apps for your phone if you prefer typing or dictation over writing. I have a journal for each of my children. When they were babies, I wrote something in their journals almost every day. Sometimes, it was just a short note; other times, it was a few pages. Now that they are older, I write less frequently, but I am still committed to writing in each of their journals on a regular basis. I love looking back through their journals and reminiscing over the stages in their first years.

To keep a journal for your child, you do not have to write every day. You can decide what schedule and what amount of writing works for you. Your baby grows so quicky, and you will forget many small steps along the way if you do not keep a record of them. You think you will remember all the little things, such as when your baby said his first word. How could you ever forget how old he was when he started crawling? Of course, you will remember how old he was when he took his first steps and when he lost his first teeth... or will you? Believe me, you will not remember all of these milestones. Write them down. Even if it is a quick bullet point list, record these events in your baby's life. There are so many small moments and highlights, and you will want to remember each one.

FINAL WORDS

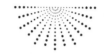

"Being a mother is learning about strengths you didn't know you had and dealing with fears you didn't know existed."

— LINDA WOOTEN

When I had my first son, it seemed like everyone had a piece of advice for me. Some advice was helpful, some not so much. However, I began to realize that most of the advice I received had a common thread: appreciate every day you have with your baby. How can so many different people be suggesting the same thing? I often heard the same phrases: "Enjoy every moment, it goes so quickly!" "Months will go by in the blink of an eye." "I miss the newborn days!" "Savor every moment." "The days are long, but the years are fast." Although I wholeheartedly agree with each of these statements, there are some days when it can be difficult to "enjoy the moment," especially when you are cleaning up someone else's bodily fluids.

Many mothers are frustrated and overwhelmed with a new baby. This is normal. In the beginning, the nights are long, and extended stretches of sleep seem far in the distant future. The time may seem to pass exceptionally slowly, especially at two in the morning. There will be times when you are exhausted and feel depleted. In these moments, remind yourself that the newborn months are *temporary*.

As a mother, you want to do everything right and be the best mom you can be, but there will be days when you doubt yourself and question many of your day-to-day decisions regarding your child. Welcome to motherhood. However, as Dr. Benjamin Spock[1] said, "Trust yourself. You know more than you think you do."

You will find, as most parents do, that the days and years seem to pick up speed as your child grows. You may be tired with a newborn, but you can also find pockets of amazement and happiness every day with your baby. Try to savor the small moments that bring you joy each day, even during the long nights, you have with your child. When you are in the thick of it, sometimes it can be difficult to feel joy. That is ok! Not every moment will bring happiness. However, focusing on gratitude and being present in the moment will help you move through the difficult times. I assure you there will be thousands of precious moments when you will look at your baby and wish you could stop time. Holding my newborn baby while he slept was one of those moments for me. There are few things more peaceful and beautiful than your baby sleeping in your arms as a newborn. The first time your baby smiles at you will pull at your heartstrings like nothing you have felt before. Feeling your baby's warm body and steady breathing against your body when you hold her close to you is a feeling you will miss as your babies grow up. These are the moments that will make a permanent impression on your heart. Take a few minutes to write down some of these moments in your journal so you remember how you felt.

Time does not stop, and your baby will change and grow every day. Take pictures and videos of your baby. Capture the special moments and the seemingly ordinary occurrences. Your baby changes faster than you can ever imagine, and you will want to look back and remember every stage of your baby's life. Take pictures of the silly, sad, frustrating moments as well as the happy moments. Someday your child will see the picture of himself screaming hysterically during his first real haircut and laugh.

Enjoy your newborn baby as much as you can every day. Appreciate this tiny person for everything that she is and will become. You have the incredible and rewarding job of introducing her to the world and helping her navigate the adventure of life. Remind yourself during the difficult moments that time goes quickly, and before you know it, you will be hugging her goodbye outside the door to the kindergarten classroom.

"Breathe. The moments matter. Not the perfect ones. But the every single day, nitty-gritty, showing-up moments of motherhood. Your kids don't need perfection. Just you. Loving, giving, trying and simply being their mom. Breathe."[2]

Be kind to yourself. As a mom, you have the most important and rewarding job in the world. Accept that each day is a new day with a unique set of challenges. Allow yourself to have personal time so you can do something that you want or need to do. Do not permit mom guilt to intrude on your goals and what you want to accomplish each day. By creating a routine that supports your needs and schedule, prioritizing sleep for both you and your baby, and taking care of yourself, you will be at your best for your baby.

THANK YOU

Thank you for reading *Navigating the Newborn Months and Beyond*. I hope the tools and strategies will help you in your motherhood journey.

If you enjoyed this book, **please leave a review on Amazon**. Reviews are vital for independent authors as they help other readers find my book and provide helpful feedback.

If you're not sure how to leave a review, please visit the Amazon Help page for assistance.

With gratitude,

Erin

NOTES

1. THE TO-DO LIST

1. Nicogossian, Claire, PsyD. 2020. *Mama, You Are Enough*. Salem, MA: Page Street Publishing.
2. Rollings, Michaela. 2020. "The Science of To-Do Lists." https://medium.com/hive-blog/the-science-of-to-do-lists-5b8371732d3b.
3. Matthews, Gail. 2015. "Goal Research Summary." Paper presented at the 9th Annual International Conference of the Psychology Research Unit of Athens Institute for Education and Research, Athens, Greece.
4. Britton, Kathryn. 2016. "Are There Items on Today's To-Do List That Bring You Joy?" *Positive Psychology News*. https://positivepsychologynews.com/news/kathryn-britton/2016071136030.
5. Miller, Sue and Delich, Holly. 2014. *Parenting is Wonder-full*. Cumming, GA: The Rethink Group, Inc.

2. YOUR DAILY SCHEDULE

1. Dahl, Melissa. Updated January 5, 2016. "Organize your to-do list from worst to best." CNN Health, Science of Us. https://edition.cnn.com/2016/01/05/health/managing-to-do-lists/index.html.
2. Dahl, Melissa. Updated January 5, 2016. "Organize your to-do list from worst to best." CNN Health, Science of Us. https://edition.cnn.com/2016/01/05/health/managing-to-do-lists/index.html.

4. UNDERSTANDING YOUR BABY'S FEEDING ROUTINE

1. Hogg, Tracy and Blau, Melinda. 2005. *The Baby Whisperer Solves All Your Problems*. New York: Atria Books.

7. THE IMPORTANCE OF A SLEEP ROUTINE FOR YOUR BABY

1. Mindell, J. A., Telofski, L. S., Wiegand, B., & Kurtz, E. S. 2009. "A nightly bedtime routine: impact on sleep in young children and maternal mood." *Sleep*, *32*(5), 599–606.
2. Dubeif, A. 2017. *Precious Little Sleep*. Lomhara Press.

8. BEDTIME ROUTINE TIP 1: SINGING TO YOUR BABY

1. Guilmartin, Kenneth K. and Levinowitz, Lili M., PhD. 2012. *Music Together, Summer Songs 1.* Princeton, NJ: Music Together LLC.
2. Persico, G., Antolini, L., Vergani, P., Costantini, W., Nardi, M. T., Bellotti, L. August 2017. "Maternal singing of lullabies during pregnancy and after birth: Effects on mother-infant bonding and on newborns' behavior. Concurrent Cohort Study." *Women and Birth,* 30, issue 4, 214-220.
3. University of Miami. 2017. "Mothers and infants connect through song." Science-Daily, 17 February. www.sciencedaily.com/releases/2017/02/170217012453.htm.
4. Cirelli, L. K., and Trehub, S. E. (2020). "Familiar songs reduce infant distress." *Developmental Psychology,* 56(5), 861– 868. https://doi.org/10.1037/dev0000917.
5. Loewy, J., Stewart, K., Dassler, A., Telsey, A., and Homel, P. 2013. "The effects of music therapy on vital signs, feeding, and sleep in premature infants." *Pediatrics, 131*(5), 902–918.
6. ECLKC, June 22, 2018. "News You Can Use: Music." https://eclkc.ohs.acf.hhs.-gov/curriculum/article/news-you-can-use-music-part-1.

9. BEDTIME ROUTINE TIP 2: READING TO YOUR BABY

1. Clevelandclinic.org, October 27, 2020. "The Benefits of Reading to Babies." *Pediatrics.*
2. American Academy of Pediatrics. 2017. "Reading with children starting in infancy gives lasting literacy boost: Shared book-reading that begins soon after birth may translate into higher language and vocabulary skills before elementary school." ScienceDaily, 4 May. www.sciencedaily.com/releases/2017/05/170504083146.htm.

10. BEDTIME ROUTINE TIP 3: SWADDLING

1. Karp, Harvey, MD. 2002. *The Happiest Baby on the Block.* Bantam.
2. Meyer, L. E., and Erler T. 2011. "Swaddling: a traditional care method rediscovered." *World J Pediatr*ics: May;7(2):155-60.
3. Weissbluth, Marc, MD. 2013. *Healthy Sleep Habits, Happy Child.* New York: Ballantine Books.
4. The Mayo Clinic defines sudden infant death syndrome (SIDS) as the unexplained death, usually during sleep, of a seemingly healthy baby less than a year old. See https://www.mayoclinic.org/diseases-conditions/sudden-infant-death-syndrome/symptoms-causes/syc-20352800.
5. Karp, Harvey, MD. 2003. *The Happiest Baby on the Block.* Bantam Books.
6. Oden, R. P., Powell, C., Sims, A., Weisman, J., Joyner, B. L., and Moon, R. Y. 2012. "Swaddling: will it get babies onto their backs for sleep?" *Clinical pediatrics, 51*(3),

254–259.

11. BEDTIME ROUTINE TIP 4: USE A PACIFIER

1. Moon R. Y., Tanabe K. O., Yang D. C., Young H. A., and Hauck F. R. 2012. "Pacifier use and SIDS: evidence for a consistently reduced risk." *Matern Child Health J.*: Apr;16(3):609-14.
2. Karp, Harvey, MD. 2012. *The Happiest Baby Guide to Great Sleep*. New York: Harper-Collins, pp. 84-85.
3. Hogg, Tracy and Blau, Melinda. 2005. *The Baby Whisperer Solves All Your Problems*. New York: Atria Books.
4. Kotlen, Melissa. 2020. "Breastfeeding and Nipple Confusion." https://www.very-wellfamily.com/nipple-confusion-431932#citation-1.
5. Karp, Harvey, MD. 2012. *The Happiest Baby Guide to Great Sleep*. New York: Harper-Collins, pp. 84.
6. Jenik, A. G., Vain, N. E., Gorestein, A. N., and Jacobi, N. E. 2009. "Does the recommendation to use a pacifier influence the prevalence of breastfeeding?" *J. Pediatr.* Sep; 155(3): 350-4e1.

12. BEDTIME ROUTINE TIP 5: WHITE NOISE

1. Healthychildren.org. 2013 "Stages of Newborn Sleep." https://www.healthychildren.org/english/ages-stages/baby/sleep/pages/phases-of-sleep.aspx.
2. The StayWell Company, LLC, medical review by Jovino, L., DO. 2010. "From Wide-Awake to Fast-Asleep: Baby's Sleep Patterns." https://www.nationwidechildrens.org/family-resources-education/family-resources-library/from-wide-awake-to-fast-asleep-babys-sleep-patterns.
3. Spencer, J. A. D., Moran, D. J., Lee, A. and Talbert, D. 1990. "White noise and sleep induction." *Archives of Disease in Childhood*, 65, no.1: (135-37).
4. Coleman-Phox, K., Odouli, R., Li, D. K. 2008. "Use of a fan during sleep and the risk of sudden infant death syndrome." *Archives of Pediatric & Adolescent Medicine*. Oct; 162(10):963-8.

13. BEDTIME ROUTINE TIP 6: DARK ROOM

1. National Institute of General Medical Sciences. 2021. "Circadian Rhythms", https://www.nigms.nih.gov/education/fact-sheets/Pages/circadian-rhythms.aspx.
2. National Institute of General Medical Sciences. 2021. "Circadian Rhythms", https://www.nigms.nih.gov/education/fact-sheets/Pages/circadian-rhythms.aspx.
3. National Center for Complementary and Integrative Health, "Melatonin, what you need to know." https://www.nccih.nih.gov/health/melatonin-what-you-need-to-know.
4. Kennedy, Janet Krone, PhD. 2015. *The Good Sleeper*. New York: Henry Holt & Company.

14. BEDTIME ROUTINE TIP 7: BEDTIME BATH

1. Haghayegh, Shahab, Khoshnevis, Sepideh, Smolensky, Michael H., Diller, Kenneth R., and Castriotta, Richard J. 2019. "Before-bedtime passive body heating by warm shower or bath to improve sleep: A systematic review and meta-analysis." *Sleep Medicine Reviews*, volume 46; August, Pages 124-135.
2. Biachi, J. 2016. "7 Secrets of a Baby Sleep Expert." https://www.jnj.com/health-and-wellness/7-secrets-baby-sleep-expert.
3. Navsaria, Dipesh, MPH, MSLIS, MD, FAAP. 2020. "Bathing Your Baby." Healthy-children.org. https://www.healthychildren.org/English/ages-stages/baby/bathing-skin-care/Pages/Bathing-Your-Newborn.aspx.

15. BEDTIME ROUTINE TIP 8: DROWSY NOT DREAMING

1. Walker, Matthew, PhD. 2017. *Why We Sleep*. New York: Scribner, 219.
2. Weissbluth, Marc, MD. 2013. *Healthy Sleep Habits, Happy Child*. New York: Ballantine Books.
3. Ferber, Richard, MD. 2006. *Solve Your Child's Sleep Problems*. New York: Fireside.

16. BEDTIME ROUTINE TIP 9: SLEEP TRAINING

1. Gary Ezzo and Robert Bucknam, M.D. *On Becoming Baby Wise.* (Louisiana, MO: Parent-Wise Solutions, Inc., 2006); Pamela Druckerman. *Bringing Up Bébé: One American Mother Discovers the Wisdom of French Parenting* (Penguin Books, 2014); Harvey Karp, M.D. *The Happiest Baby Guide to Great Sleep.* (New York: Harper-Collins Publishers, 2012); Marc Weissbluth, M.D. *Healthy Sleep Habits, Happy Child.* (New York: Ballantine Books, 2003); Richard Ferber, M.D. *Solve Your Child's Sleep Problems.* (New York: Fireside, 2006).

17. TOOLS TO REDUCE FUSSINESS

1. Kristensen, I. H., Simonsen, M., Trillingsgaard, T., Pontoppidan, M., and Kronborg, H. 2018. "First-time mothers' confidence, mood, and stress in the first months postpartum. A cohort study." Sex Reprod Healthc. Oct; 17:43-49. doi: 10.1016/j.srhc.2018.06.003. Epub 2018 Jun 25. PMID: 30193719.
2. Murkoff, Heidi, Mazel, Sharon, Eisenberg, Arlene, Hathaway, Sandee, BSN. 2003. *What to Expect the First Year.* New York: Workman Publishing Company Inc., pp. 556-559.
3. Cirelli, L. K., and Trehub, S. E. 2020. "Familiar songs reduce infant distress." *Developmental Psychology, 56*(5), 861–868. https://doi.org/10.1037/dev0000917.
4. Mariève Corbeil, Sandra E. and Trehub, Isabelle Peretz. 2015. "Singing Delays the Onset of Infant Distress." *Infancy*; DOI: 10.1111/infa.12114.

5. Mariève Corbeil, Sandra E. and Trehub, Isabelle Peretz. 2015. "Singing Delays the Onset of Infant Distress." *Infancy*; DOI: 10.1111/infa.12114.

18. CALMING YOUR FUSSY BABY WITH MOVEMENT AND CONNECTION

1. Halsey, Claire, ClinPsyD. 2012. *Baby Development, Everything You Need to Know*. New York: DK Publishing, 2012.
2. Murkoff, Heidi, Mazel, Sharon, Eisenberg, Arlene, Hathaway, Sandee, BSN. 2003. *What to Expect the First Year*. New York: Workman Publishing Company Inc., pp. 304-305.

19. NAPS

1. Dhand, R., and Sohal, H. 2006. "Good sleep, bad sleep! The role of daytime naps in healthy adults." *Current opinion in pulmonary medicine, 12*(6), 379–382. https://doi.org/10.1097/01.mcp.0000245703.92311.d0.

20. NIGHTTIME SLEEP

1. Pacheco, Danielle. 2020. "Alcohol and Sleep." https://www.sleepfoundation.org/nutrition/alcohol-and-sleep.
2. National Institute of Mental Health. "Perinatal Depression", NIH Publication No. 20-MH-8116, https://www.nimh.nih.gov/health/publications/perinatal-depression/.

21. EXERCISE

1. Roy, Brad A., PhD, FACSM, 2014. "Postpartum Exercise." *American College of Sports Medicine's Health & Fitness Journal*. Volume 18, issue 6: 3-4. doi: 10.1249/FIT.0000000000000071.
2. Bruce, Debrah Fulghum, PhD. 2020. "Exercise and Depression." https://www.webmd.com/depression/guide/exercise-depression.
3. Center for Disease Control and Prevention. 2021. "Benefits of Physical Activity." https://www.cdc.gov/physicalactivity/basics/pa-health/index.htm.
4. Roy, Brad A., PhD, FACSM, 2014. "Postpartum Exercise." *American College of Sports Medicine's Health & Fitness Journal*. Volume 18, issue 6: 3-4. doi: 10.1249/FIT.0000000000000071.
5. Harvard Health Publishing. "Exercise and Fitness." https://www.health.harvard.edu/topics/exercise-and-fitness.
6. American College of Obstetricians and Gynecologists. 2019. "Exercise After Pregnancy." https://www.acog.org/Patients/FAQs/Exercise-After-Pregnancy?IsMobileSet=false#start.

7. Barton, Jo and Pretty, Jules 2010. "What is the best dose of nature and green exercise for improving mental health? A multi-study analysis." *Environmental Science and Technology*, 44, 10, 3947–3955.

8. Barton, Jo and Pretty, Jules 2010. "What is the best dose of nature and green exercise for improving mental health? A multi-study analysis." *Environmental Science and Technology*, 44, 10, 3947–3955.

9. Scaccia, Annamarya. 2020. "Is a Vitamin D Deficiency Causing Your Depression?" https://www.healthline.com/health/depression-and-vitamin-d.

10. Duke Medicine. "Parenting and home environment influence children's exercise and eating habits." ScienceDaily. www.sciencedaily.com/releases/2013/06/130618113652.htm (accessed August 8, 2021).

22. HYDRATION

1. An, R. and McCaffrey, J. 2016. "Plain Water Consumption in Relation to Energy Intake and Diet Quality Among US Adults, 2005-2012." *Journal of Human Nutrition and Dietetics*, 29 (5), pp. 624-632.

2. Harvard Medical School. September 2016, updated March 25, 2020. "How much water should you drink?" Harvard Health Publishing.

3. Mayo Clinic Staff. 2020. "Water: How much should you drink every day?" Mayo Clinic, Healthy Lifestyle, Nutrition and Healthy Eating. https://www.mayoclinic.org/healthy-lifestyle/nutrition-and-healthy-eating/in-depth/water/art-20044256.

23. SOCIAL INTERACTION

1. Gurevich, Rachel, R. N. 2020. "Why You're Feeling Isolated as a New Mom." Very Well Family. https://www.verywellfamily.com/why-you-re-feeling-isolated-as-a-new-mom-and-what-to-do-4769084.

2. https://www.lasmadres.org/

3. McMaster University. 2012. "Babies' brains benefit from music lessons, even before they can walk and talk." *ScienceDaily*, 9 May. www.sciencedaily.com/releases/2012/05/120509123653.htm.

4. Sigmundsson, H. and Hopkins, B. 2010. "Baby swimming: exploring the effects of early intervention on subsequent motor abilities." *Child Care Health Dev.* 36:3, 428-430. DOI: 10.1111/j.1365-2214.2009.00990.x.

5. Stewart, Darienne Hosley. "When can my baby go on a park swing?" BabyCenter.com, https://www.babycenter.com/baby-activities-play/when-can-my-baby-go-on-a-park-swing_1368522.

25. JOURNALING

1. University of Rochester Medical Center. "Journaling for Mental Health."

2. Baikie, Karen A. and Wilhem, Kay. 2005. "Emotional and Physical Health Benefits of Expressive Writing." *Advances in Psychiatric Treatment* 11(5), 338-346.

3. Pennebaker, J. W., Kiecolt-Glaser, J. K., and Glaser, R. 1988. "Disclosure of traumas and immune function: Health implications for psychotherapy." *Journal of Consulting and Clinical Psychology*, Vol. 56, pp. 239-245.
4. Pennebaker, J. W., Kiecolt-Glaser, J. K., and Glaser, R. 1988. "Disclosure of traumas and immune function: Health implications for psychotherapy." *Journal of Consulting and Clinical Psychology*, Vol. 56, pp. 239-245.
5. Smyth, J. M., Stone, A. A., Hurewitz, A., and Kaell, A. 1999. "Effects of Writing About Stressful Experiences on Symptom Reduction in Patients With Asthma or Rheumatoid Arthritis: A Randomized Trial." *JAMA*;281(14):1304–1309.
6. Barth, F. Diane. 2020. "Journaling isn't just good for mental health. It might also help your physical health." https://www.nbcnews.com/think/opinion/journaling-isn-t-just-good-mental-health-it-might-also-ncna1114571.
7. Eurich, Tasha. 2018. "What Self-Awareness Really Is (and how to cultivate it)." *Harvard Business Review*. https://hbr.org/2018/01/what-self-awareness-really-is-and-how-to-cultivate-it.

FINAL WORDS

1. Dr. Benjamin Spock was an American pediatrician who was widely recognized for his best-selling book *Baby and Child Care* which was published in 1946.
2. Rachel Marie Martin, creator of findingjoy.net https://findingjoy.net/ and author of The Brave Art of Motherhood.

ACKNOWLEDGMENTS

To Curtis, my husband of twenty-one years, thank you for quietly supporting me and respecting my space throughout my writing process without ever interfering, reading my writing, or asking too many questions.

Thank you to my dear friend and accomplished author, Sally Miller, for your encouragement and invaluable advice.

Many, many thanks to my brilliant editor, Jessica Andersen, whose attention to detail is unparalleled. Jessica is my second set of eyes and always brings an honest, positive approach to improving my writing skills.

Thank you, Mom, for always believing in me and supporting me.

I am beyond grateful for my four beautiful children who supported and encouraged me throughout my writing process. Greysen, thank you for being my personal cheerleader, secretly reading over my shoulder, and always checking my word count on a daily (sometimes hourly) basis.

ABOUT THE AUTHOR

I am the proud mother of four beautiful children, three sons and one daughter, all of whom are energetic, creative, engaging, and loud. I am married to my college sweetheart, a patient, generous, intelligent, golf-obsessed man who makes me laugh and shares my love of the outdoors.

I was born and raised in the northwest suburbs of Chicago, Illinois where I endured many freezing winters with below-zero windchill. I attended Vanderbilt University in Nashville, Tennessee for my undergraduate education, where I competed in Division 1 cross country and track and field for four years. I attended Loyola University Chicago School of Law where I received my J.D. Prior to having children, I practiced health care law at two different law firms and most recently worked for the Office of the General Counsel at Stanford University. I enjoy swimming, running, hiking, biking, playing the piano, and spending time outdoors with my children. I keep my sanity by reading, writing, and enjoying the beauty of Northern California as much as possible every day.

The idea to write this book began forming over four years ago. After my fourth child transitioned to the toddler phase, I found myself bursting with ideas and information about babies and a desire to capture my thoughts and share them with other moms. In 2020, a year that involved frustration, sadness, and isolation due to a worldwide pandemic, I found my own joy and purpose in creating this book. Writing it has been an incredible personal journey for which I am grateful every day.

Navigating the Newborn Months and Beyond is my first book. You can learn more about me and my writing by visiting my website at http://erineileenleigh.com.

Made in the USA
Las Vegas, NV
02 May 2022

48319898R10075